Clear Skies, Deep Water

Clear Skies, Deep Water

A Chautauqua Memoir

BETH PEYTON

excelsior editions

State University of New York Press
Albany, New York

Cover photo courtesy of Beth Peyton

Published by State University of New York Press, Albany

© 2014 State University of New York

Excelsior Editions is an imprint of State University of New York Press

For information, contact State University of New York Press, Albany, NY
www.sunypress.edu

Production by Diane Ganeles
Marketing by Kate McDonnell

Library of Congress Cataloging-in-Publication Data

Peyton, Beth, 1956–
    Clear skies, deep water : a Chautauqua memoir / Beth Peyton.
        pages cm — (Excelsior editions)
    ISBN 978-1-4384-5172-5 (pbk. : alk. paper)
    1. Peyton, Beth, 1956– 2. Peyton, Beth, 1956—-Homes and haunts—New
York—Chautauqua Lake Region. 3. Chautauqua Lake Region (N.Y.)—Social
life and customs. 4. Chautauqua Lake Region (N.Y.)—Biography. I. Title.

F127.C7P49 2014
974.7'95—dc23   2013025551

10 9 8 7 6 5 4 3 2 1

For those we've lost, and all we've found

Contents

Acknowledgments

Thank you to all of the wonderful family, friends, and neighbors who have been with me—with us—along this journey, through thick and thin. Those included in the book were chosen because they supported the narrative, not because of their importance in my life then, or now. Thank you for sharing your memories, your photographs, your stories, and for letting us in.

I am truly indebted to the faculty, staff, guest writers, and my chums from Carlow University's low-residency M.F.A. program. Under the firm guidance of Director Ellie Wymard, PhD, I was blessed to study with both Irish and American writers. The Carlow community was beside me as I walked a pretty dark path, always pulling me toward beauty. They are beside me still. I am grateful for the ringing language of the Irish, and for that glorious sky that helped me see my own sky more clearly. Thank you for helping me persevere.

Jane Candia Coleman, my manuscript mentor and dear friend, helped me find my voice. In writing for her, I learned how to write for myself.

Thank you to Kathy Cherry, artist extraordinaire, who captured my story and the spirit of the lake in her wonderful maps.

I would be remiss if I did not acknowledge those involved with the literary arts at The Chautauqua Institution. Their celebration and support of reading and writing have helped me never forget the importance of books. The Institution is my center for lifelong learning, and just a quick boat ride away.

Thank you to Amanda Lanne, my Acquisitions Editor, Diane Ganeles, my Production Editor, Kate McDonnell, my Marketing Manager, and the rest of the staff at SUNY Press. I am truly grateful for their support, dedication, professionalism, and friendship. They made this process a blast.

Thank you most of all to my husband, Jeff Hunter, for being fully present and for having the courage and humor to live this life with me.

A version of "Karaoke Night at the Casino" appeared in *The Jamestown Post-Journal* January 28, 2012.

Prologue

I live on Chautauqua Lake. I love the way the word *Chautau-qua* rolls off my tongue, the hard and soft sounds of it. Visitors describe the place as quaint, but I can feel a more ancient spirit here sometimes—a spirit at least as old as the name *Chautauqua* itself—just beneath the surface.

The dictionary defines *Chautauqua* as any outdoor summer meeting, but the movement that swept the nation around the turn of the nineteenth century, providing education combined with popular entertainment, lectures, concerts, and plays, started here, on Chautauqua Lake, in Western New York State. The name *Chautauqua* is derived from the Seneca language and most commonly is thought to mean "a bag tied in the middle," or "two moccasins fastened together." With its upper and lower basins cinched together between Bemus Point and Stow, on a map Chautauqua Lake does look like it's tied in the middle. As with everything else here, there is more than one story, and as a result, both the meaning and derivation of the name have been debated. The word *Chautauqua* may actually be derived from the Cherokee, and may also mean "the place where one was lost," "foggy place," or "the place where the fish was taken out." To me, Chautauqua is all these things—and more.

Since the late 1800s, Chautauqua Lake has been a vacation destination point for the wealthy from New York City, Pittsburgh, Buffalo, and Cleveland. Located in the southwesternmost corner of New York State, the lake is large, over seventeen miles long, with a surface area of thirteen thousand acres. With an elevation over thirteen hundred feet, Chautauqua is one of the highest navigable waterways in the world. Even though it is in close proximity to Cleveland, Pittsburgh, and Buffalo, it has the feel and climate of a mountain lake, and is a good place to beat the summer heat.

On the map, the lake looks like a misplaced Finger Lake. Although it is not considered part of New York State's Finger Lake system, it was formed by the same glacial mass as the Finger Lakes. They were carved when the glaciers came down, while Chautauqua was made when the glaciers retreated. The glacial activity left a wonderful layer of rich topsoil, in addition to a beautiful lake, and despite the cool climate and long winters, the vegetation and foliage are lush and green. The old-fashioned things look best here: hydrangeas, lilacs, roses, and rhododendrons. The cemeteries and the gardens in some of the old places contain tree hydrangeas, an heirloom variety with an upright habit, covered with heavy flower heads throughout the summer and fall. The blossoms weigh the trees down as they turn from white to pink, to rust, and finally, to the color of linen. The dried flowers provide winter interest in dining rooms, on porches, and in dormant gardens. Irises bloom in perennial gardens and grow wild along the creek beds, and in the spring, the roadsides are covered with white, pink, and purple phlox. Gladiolas burst forth in fields in late July. Buckets filled with cut glads ring the lake and grace porches until Labor Day, a sign of welcome.

Locally grown fruits and vegetables are sold at stands all summer long and into the fall. Regular truck garden produce—tomatoes, onions, squash, melons, corn, and beans—is abundant. Peaches, apples, blueberries, strawberries, and even figs are available, although the fig trees must winter under shelter. The area is famous for its grapes. Concord grapes and little champagne grapes are the most common, and many growers in the area supply grapes for Welch's, which has a plant in Westfield, just over a big hill from Chautauqua on Lake Erie. Local wineries are beginning to experiment with vinifera grapes but have a long way to go to catch up with wineries in the Finger Lakes that are producing truly exceptional wines, both white and red.

Trees are tapped to make maple syrup and other products, like maple cream, unsurpassed as a topping for toast, at least in our family. I'm not much for sweets, but something about maple cream is irresistible. Although the only ingredient in maple cream is maple syrup, the process of heating and whipping the syrup to make the spun cream brings out a nutty flavor, and to me, it tastes as if I were eating both the syrup and something of the woody tree at the same time. Maple products are for sale at several stands, sometimes on the honor system where scuffed coins and crumpled bills are left in a coffee can.

The largest population center on Chautauqua Lake is the city of Jamestown, known chiefly for manufacturing furniture out of the maple, cherry, oak, and other hardwood trees that circle the lake and cover the hills beyond, in addition to its claim as the birthplace of Lucille Ball. The rest of the lake is ringed by hamlets and villages of various sizes, including Bemus Point, where the old ferry still runs, connecting with Stow at the narrowest part of the lake; Mayville at the north end; and Celoron at the south end. Born in Jamestown, Lucille Ball spent much of her youth in Celoron, and which town can rightly claim her is a sticking point among the locals. Point Chautauqua is a residential community designed by Frederick Law Olmsted, of Central Park fame, and Midway Park, a small amusement park located next to Maple Springs, was established in 1889 and is still operational.

Chautauqua Lake is perhaps most noted for The Chautauqua Institution. Started in 1884 as an "experiment in vacation learning" for Methodist Sunday school teachers, the Institution, as it is known, is another little hamlet on the lake with its own zip code and just a handful of full-time residents. During the summer season, the place is a thriving pedestrian community, drawing thousands of people from around the world. While the Institution is loosely organized around a lecture series that covers broad topics such as peace, justice, leadership, literature, global conflict, and the future, religion still plays a fundamental role there, with daily worship services at the big amphitheater on the grounds.

Several presidents and various other American movers and shakers have come to the Chautauqua Institution. Thomas Edison married the daughter of one of Chautauqua's founders and spent many summers here. Other noted visitors have included Amelia Earhart, Admiral Byrd, Henry Ford, and George Gershwin. Around the turn of the century, the Chautauqua model for education and dialogue was so highly regarded that "tent Chautauquas" sprang up all over the country. These portable Chautauquas dwindled after the proliferation of the automobile and radio, but the Institution has survived and is still thriving. While a smattering of other "Chautauquas" still exist, none is so large or well-reputed as the original.

Old Victorian houses with cottage gardens line the quaint streets of the Institution. Some are individually owned and passed down through the generations; others are owned by churches or clubs, communally shared among members; still others have been converted to apartments or condominiums, yet retain their original cottage looks. Parks and green spaces dot the landscape, and Bestor Plaza, the hub of the Institution, is meticulously landscaped and impeccably manicured. A bookstore, a library, shops, hotels, and restaurants line the square. On the lakefront, a swimming beach, cottages, and the bell tower, along with the striking façade of the old Athenaeum Hotel, provide a backdrop to the large dock and recreation center.

Even though the Institution was designed to be a utopian ideal, it can be a little restrained. With its focus on morality and higher purpose, for most of its existence the Institution was dry. Not only was liquor not for sale on the grounds, it could not be imbibed. As a result, the ladies who gathered on wide porches in the evening sipped their gin out of teacups to fool the Temperance Society: Chautauqua tea. Even today there is no liquor store or bar on the grounds.

Theodore Roosevelt called Chautauqua "the most American thing in America," and William Jennings Bryan said that Chautauqua and its traveling versions were "a potent human factor in molding the mind of the nation." But Chautauqua was not without its critics. Sinclair Lewis called it "nothing but wind and chaff and . . . the laughter of yokels." Composer and music critic Gregory Mason said being at Chautauqua was "infinitely easier than trying to think." And after being initially charmed, psychologist William James wrote that "this order is too tame, this culture too second-rate, this goodness too uninspiring. This human drama without a villain or a pang; this community so refined that ice-cream soda-water is the utmost offering it can make to the brute animal in man . . . this atrocious harmlessness of all things, I cannot abide with them. . . ."

"Feh!" our neighbor George Whitbeck said about the Institution. "I won't go over there anymore. You get there early to get your concert seats, then all the old people come cramming in ten minutes before it starts. They don't even say 'excuse me.' They just squish you in like a sardine."

I don't mind the crowding, but, although I'm a lifelong avid reader, I find the bookishness there a bit creepy. Half the people in a Chautauqua concert audience have their heads in books before it starts, and some read all the way through the performance. It's like those parents who participate in their children's lives only through the lens of a video camera. All they see is through the frame, and everything feels staged. In my opinion, it would be a sin to allow a book—any book—to come between me and the still-elfin magic of Ian Anderson at a Jethro Tull concert, even if it is held on the hallowed grounds of the Chautauqua Amphitheater. My husband, Jeff, like Thomas Edison, enjoys some of the activities but would rather go fishing than hear people talk all day. Still, the criticism seems overly harsh for this wonderful and unique place that we're fortunate enough to be able to enjoy.

It was the hamlet of Maple Springs, on the opposite shore from the Institution, that pulled us in and anchored us on Chautauqua Lake. This old-fashioned place comforted us, restored us, and gave us a sense of hope and renewal during one of the darkest times in our lives.

Maple Springs was established around 1880, with the post office run out of a hotel, and like the more famous Institution, has a storied history as well. Some of it shows up in regional publications, and in books published in the "Images of America" series: the sepia-toned local histories of little burgs all over the United States. Perhaps the most interesting histories are oral histories: stories passed around the fire pits, or those captured by Sandy McClain and Nancy Sweeney, who compiled *The Legend of Maple Springs*.

Although filled in with factoids and information gathered elsewhere, *The Legend of Maple Springs*, photocopied and distributed throughout the community since 1977, resulted from interviews with a resident named Maurice Bosworth. He moved here as a child in 1908; his father ran the general store, and Maurice lived here all his life. *The Legend* says that Maurice was a general merchant, general contractor, real estate broker, and town tax assessor. The history is filled with recollections of his life in Maple Springs and contains a good record of the history and ownership transfers of all the houses and buildings. One must be steeped in Maple Springs lore and geography to understand a word of it because there are so many references to where things used to be, or to specific houses, like "the house known as the Chandley Girls' house that Ivy Fleming lives in now," or "Robert Rawsthorn who was the father of Bertha Lowe who owns the house, second one to the right on the bank beyond the bridge."

Old Maple Springs was filled with boarding houses, hotels, vacation and fishing cottages, and icehouses. People made their living serving the tourism industry. Some local residents filled steamships with water from several ponds. There was a sawmill here, and big docks for the steamships. Travelers arrived for the summer with heavy steamer trunks; according to Mr. Bosworth, the heavier the trunk, the higher up in the hotel they went. People "put up ice," thick slabs of blue ice (free of snow) and white ice, stored it in icehouses, and shipped it out by train to Pittsburgh. The Jamestown, Chautauqua Lake and Erie Railroad circled the lake. It was known as the JCLE, which the locals said stood for "Jesus Christ's Last Effort." Later on, the railway company changed the name to the Jamestown, Westfield, and Northwestern Interurban Line. The locals called it the JW and NW, or by its more colorful name, "Jesus Wept and No Wonder."

A lot has changed in Maple Springs since its heyday in the early 1900s, but much has remained the same. In 1959, when Spike and Norma Kelderhouse bought the Whiteside Hotel for twelve thousand dollars, it had been a vacation destination point since the turn of the century. Situated on the lakefront, the hotel had forty guest rooms, a large dining room, tennis and shuffle-board courts, and an old-fashioned ambiance reminiscent of the days when Saratoga-style hotels circled the lake and people took trolleys, trains, and steamships to their destinations.

Spike and Norma grew up on the lake. Spike graduated from Bemus High School in Bemus Point, and together they operated a charter fishing business. After they bought the hotel, Spike continued to take people fishing, while Norma worked like hell to keep the hotel running and keep her eye on their eight children.

The view from the hotel porch was spectacular. Just past a circular drive, the treed lawn gently sloped down to the lakefront. In 1959 there was only one big dock, although canoes, fishing skiffs, and rowboats were pulled up on shore. Unobstructed views of the sunset could be taken in at the shoreline or at the end of the dock, and the bell tower from the Chautauqua Institution could be seen across the lake. The opposite shore was lined with trees and vibrant green lawns, and on sunny days the blue lake reflected the deep blue sky.

Spike and Norma sold the Whiteside Hotel in 1984. They simply could not afford to install a sprinkler system and bring it up to code. It was the last hotel in Maple Springs, and one of the last three old hotels standing on the lake. A developer built the townhouses, a two-story six-plex, in 1988.

I wasn't here in 1959—I was a baby in Nebraska—but I know what they saw, and not just from the pictures. For the past fifteen years I've been looking at the same view, as a guest at a bed and breakfast just down the road, and as a part-time resident in one of those townhouses built on the same plot of land where the hotel sat. The big dock is gone now, but the concrete footings that held it are still here, and the large trees that shaded the lawn of the hotel remain.

The view through the sliding glass door of our townhouse is the same view as from the hotel, though now several docks pepper the lakefront in place of the large dock that served the hotel. George Whitbeck was at the lakefront at dawn the day the hotel came down, to put in his own dock. Even though the townhouse residents are all second- or third-generation owners, there are people who still resent the loss of the hotel and somehow blame the townhouse owners for its demise. Change doesn't come easily to an old-timey place like this.

Maple Springs remains a tourist community. People still own cottages and spend their summers at the lake, and many people rent cottages or stay at the bed and breakfast for a few days or weeks. The kids walk down to Midway Park to ride the rides or play skeeball. People fish or boat, attend classes, concerts, events, and lectures at the Institution, go to restaurants, walk around, catch up on their reading. They sit around fire pits and roast s'mores or popcorn, drink beer, and tell stories. The general store is open again, only now as an antique store, art studio, and post office. Worms are for sale there, too, on the same honor system used to sell produce or maple cream. The worms are in an outside fridge, with the money left in a jar in the freezer.

Although the winter traffic can be brisk with snowmobilers, ice fishermen, and skiers, only a handful of people live year-round in Maple Springs. These locals, as in the old days, make their livings doing a variety of things, as Maurice Bosworth did. People sell real estate, run businesses, paint houses, guide hunting and fishing trips, winterize cottages, mow lawns, plow snow, sell produce, build things, fix things, quilt, hook rugs, write. What binds us, the full-timers and the part-timers, the old and the young, is the beauty of the lake, along with something deeper, perhaps ancient and tribal, something unexpressed.

I heard some stories about Maurice Bosworth, that legend of Maple Springs—stories that weren't recorded by Sandy and Nancy. I heard that he opened and closed seasonal cottages for people, and if they didn't use him, or didn't shop at the general store he ran, he would raise their taxes, since he was also the tax assessor. I heard he was in the maple syrup business as well, but never gave Norma Kelderhouse a discount on syrup even though she bought loads of it for the hotel and the syrup was tapped from her own trees.

"My parents would go up to the sugar shack with their friends," Kathie McCarthy told me. "And Maurice would make them some concoction from maple syrup, rum, and snow. They would be completely snockered when they got home."

I heard that he showed George and Sandra Whitbeck a lovely house one time when they were interested in renting a place in

Maple Springs. Years later, George met the fellow who owned the house, and he told George that the house had been in his family for generations and had *never* been available to rent. Apparently, Bosworth just let himself in the open door and showed them around.

"My dad looked at a cottage when he was up here visiting," Ren Collins told us one evening. "He decided to buy it, but there was a problem. The owner had just signed a year-long rental agreement with someone. My dad went to see Maurice at the store to see what he could work out, because Maurice was the realtor. My dad explained the situation about the renter. Maurice just reached around and pulled the agreement out of the mailbox, because he was the postmaster, too."

The stories about Maurice Bosworth might just be gossip, but I've learned that if I hear a story, or a version of it, more than once, from more than one person, it's usually at least partly true. And if it's a good story, I might just repeat it, perhaps improving upon it in the telling.

My husband, Jeff, and I recently started a new chapter in our lives. In part because of the downturn in the economy, we decided to make Chautauqua Lake, and Maple Springs in particular, our permanent home. We're locals now. We sold our family home and our townhouse, with its spectacular view, and moved seven houses away, to a house built in 1916 by Maurice Bosworth's father. The Bosworths lived there until 1922, and it has changed hands several times since. We're still in the process of improving it, and probably always will be, but it has lovely bones, a big yard, and with some of the old landscaping torn down, a view of the lake. Our new neighbor, Steve, who lives next door in the old fire hall, reminded us not to tell the tax assessor about our view or the taxes will go up. It is already starting to feel like home.

Chautauqua Lake

N

Mayville

Chautauqua Belle

Mar. Mar.

Point Chautauqua

Rt. 430

Haff Acres PIES

Chautauqua Institution

Viking Lodge

Midway Park

Maple Springs

We Wan Chu.

Rt. 394

Long Point

See Zurh House

NYC 440 miles

Bemus Point

Stow

Erie

Casino

Cheney Pt.

Route 430

Lakewood

BIG TREE Maple Products

Celoron Home of Lucille Ball

Jamestown

Not for navigation ◆ Not to scale

Cheng

Maple Springs
- on -
Chautauqua Lake

Winter

I prefer winter and fall, when you feel the bone structure of
the landscape—the loneliness of it, the dead feeling of winter.
Something waits beneath it, the whole story doesn't show.

—Andrew Wyeth

Even during the summers in Maple Springs, at the height of the
tourist season, it is so quiet that if you walk at night after ten
o'clock, you can sometimes hear people snoring through their window screens. The water gently laps the shore; it is rhythmic and
soothing and lulls us to sleep. But in the winter, it is so quiet
you can sometimes hear the snow fall. Not just during a storm,
when the snow is hard and icy, but during those beautiful snows
where the soft, fat flakes drift gently down. If I listen carefully, I
can hear them land on the snow-covered ground with a tiny pat.

Last year, Jeff and I spent our first winter at the lake as
full-time residents, living in our townhouse, working on our new
house, and waiting for spring. We were settling in, even though
we were still very unsettled. We bided our time, moving forward

slowly and with purpose, trying to pay attention. The path that brought us here was bumpy, but we let the lake work its magic on us as it's done for years. We let the lake restore us as we restored a neglected old house.

We bought the house at the end of the summer. Built in 1916, it's an old craftsman-style, just off the lake. It's a cottage, although it has a full basement. Around here, people call their houses cottages, although technically a cottage doesn't have a foundation or central heat, and can be lived in only seasonally. Our cottage was so overgrown and unremarkable that when we heard it was for sale I could not place it, although I'd walked or driven past it hundreds, maybe thousands, of times. Untrimmed spirea, forsythia, and other weedy shrubs hid the fence, a gate, a sidewalk; a hedge of yews grew up over the entire porch. Inside, it had every ugly finish invented: awful paneling, Masonite, and that plastic wall covering usually seen only in mobile homes. Filthy carpeting covered the floors, and shelving, stacked with boxes, hid the beauty of the porches and marred many of the rooms. Doors led nowhere; sidewalks were covered over by gardens mulched with newspaper, magazines, and discarded Bibles.

Old houses seem to take two paths. If the original owners took care of the house, if they showed enough love and weren't imperiled by disaster, the house was passed down to like-minded owners. But if the original owners abused the house, it was passed on to other house abusers. The house next door was occupied by successive long stretches of loving owners, and still has the original wainscoting and pristine plaster walls. Ours suffered from short, sometimes long, bursts of neglectors. There was at least one foreclosure. The house was hideous, but had potential, potential that we unearthed inch by cruddy inch.

They call it the Mitchell house. A family by a different name lived in it for the last thirty years, and another family before that, but it's still the Mitchell house in the neighborhood vernacular. Many of the locals have vivid memories of the house in times past: the window seat, the plum trees that grew along the fence line, the French doors that separated the living room from the dining room, now long gone. Almost every new visitor, those snoopy people who wondered what the hell we were doing in there, added a nugget of house history to what we already knew. Storied, that's what the house is.

An enclosed porch runs across the entire front of the house. We think that half of the porch was originally open, so entry was onto an open but covered porch, then onto the enclosed side of the porch to the front door. That door opens into a large room, long and wide, for both living and dining, with a window seat at one end and a colorful flagstone fireplace at the other. There is a parlor off this room, through French doors. At one time it served as a beauty parlor, and though we'll use it as a den, we'll always call it the beauty parlor. The fireplace had been neglected along with everything else. The cost of fixing it to burn wood was prohibitive, so we had a gas stove installed. The stove looks like it belongs and efficiently heats the main level—I didn't want to mess with all the wood anyway. The hearth is concrete, with a lovely old patina that my fireplace guy says is just dirt, but I like it and have mixed feelings about trying to scrub it off. An outline of a maple leaf is pressed into each corner, and they're what ultimately sold me. Maple leaves from ancient trees that grew or might still be growing in Maple Springs are permanently etched into my hearth. Leaves from trees that may have been here since the Civil War, or before. My urge to claim them was sharp and strong.

The work on the house was painstakingly slow, and we tried to do as much of it ourselves as we could. Jeff is an excellent carpenter, and has a wide range of other construction skills, so he was able to replace the wiring and a lot of the plumbing himself. He knocked down walls, moved doorways, framed in bathrooms and ceilings, added insulation. I painted and supervised. We'd remodeled together before, and things generally went pretty smoothly. They got testy only if I thought Jeff was infringing on the decorative aspects of the house or trying to tell me how I'd use my new kitchen. He got irritated at me if he thought I was intruding into construction territory, or if something I wanted would require too much work. Things went surprisingly well, actually, given what we'd been through. Our mojo is slowly returning; our planets are settling back into their celestial paths.

We got knocked off course when, in the span of a year, we lost both of our mothers and Jeff's business. I'd been primary caregiver for Jeff's mother for several years, and it was difficult watching her physical and mental decline. She had frequent emergencies, and just when I would begin to feel like I could move forward with my own life, another hospitalization or event would happen. I felt like a character in *High Anxiety,* that silly Mel Brooks movie, stretched taut and thin. Just when I felt ready to snap, I got the call that my own mother, considerably younger than Jeff's and until then active and healthy, was gravely ill. My mother, the wrong mother, died, the economy tanked, Jeff shut his business down, and then his mother died. For Jeff, losing the business was perhaps the worst death of all. We wandered around stunned like zombies. Individually and collectively we were almost in too much pain to move. Each of us was so depleted, we had nothing to give, but each of us was beyond comfort anyway. Watching each other suffer was almost unbearable. We were each in our own sad world, and wanted to jump off, fly away.

During that awful time, we came to the lake to rest and recharge ourselves as often as we could. We moved through a thick fog until we decided to relocate permanently to Chautauqua Lake, to try to put our lives back together, certain to be in a place we loved, and certain of nothing else.

The summer was lovely, but somehow we needed the winter. During winter, the color of the lake is stripped of its vibrancy. The view through the townhouse windows was all whites, grays, and watery blues: gray tree trunks running to black, dark gray hills on the opposite shore, and white-gray skies. Dock stanchions and sections were stacked on the lakefront amid the scattered boatlifts, and the bare trees stood out in bas-relief, in stark contrast yet enveloped by the white and the gray. We walked this muted landscape, resting our weary hearts and minds, holding still and gathering strength, waiting for our future to be revealed.

We'd seen the lake freeze before. One year, at Christmas, we went to bed with the waves and wind roiling and racketing; by morning, the lake was frozen and still. We felt a hush as water and air movement ceased. The birds gathered like tribes on top of the solid blackness they had swum and fished in just the day before, the blue-gray ice crystals transformed into still black water.

I've watched other bodies of water freeze, with the ice forming at the shoreline and working its way out, but this lake freezes differently. Here, when the conditions are right, the top layer of water suddenly reaches the right temperature and the whole surface freezes as the crystals merge to form a solid sheet of ice. The expanse of frozen stillness was astonishing. It was suddenly so quiet I could hear the ruffle of a bird's feathers in the neighbor's tree, the pat pat pat of gentle snowfall, and my own heartbeat.

Those of us who are lucky bury our parents. It's just part of life, and while it is difficult, most of us muddle through. For us, it wasn't the events themselves that were so difficult, although they were. It was perhaps because they happened within such a short time span that we lost our bearings. I call it our fifty-car pile-up, and it did feel like that. We just kept getting knocked down and down and down.

But the swing of the sledgehammer, the noise of the hammer drill, the smell of freshly sawn wood, even the swirling plaster dust began to heal us. We started tentatively, each of us secretly knowing that the longer it took to finish the house, the longer we could delay coming to terms with our uncertain future. We knew we'd have to get back on our feet, but didn't know how. We're still unsure, but somehow the future is here.

Our first winter as residents was spectacular in its harshness. The lake froze before Christmas, and it froze rough. The freezing didn't wait for the waves and wind to calm, but captured them in their full force, waves in motion set in ice. We had over seventeen feet of snowfall—a lot of snow by any standard—although we recently learned that's about the average around here. The snow, light and fluffy when it fell, heavy when it began to melt, crushed the windshield on our boat and shattered the glass on my patio table.

But we were strengthened by the quietness of winter, and by the eagles. They visit the lakefront occasionally to fish near the mouths of creeks and streams, then retreat to the woodsy hills beyond our sightline. We were strengthened by the trumpeter swans who flew through on their way south. They were regal on the lake, and electric in their whiteness against the white sky while in flight. The lake was still frozen and the ground covered with snow when the birds started singing their spring songs, their nesting songs, even as we sang ours.

The pull of the lake is strong. It's an old song that runs ancient and deep through me. I listened and waited for spring.

We Are Introduced to the Lake

She explained that she had not lost her way, but that she was
trying to find a convenient dry nesting-place.

—Jemima Puddle Duck (Beatrix Potter)

The way I first saw the lake is still my favorite way to see it. Taking
the New York Southern Tier Expressway from just outside Erie,
Pennsylvania, I couldn't see the lake until we crested the bridge,
and then I saw shining blue water extending to both horizons.
From the bridge, which bisects the lake in the middle, we could
see green lawns, cottages, the old ferry, and The Village Casino. The
lake met the green shoreline and, on the horizon, touched the blue
sky. The view was breathtaking, and even more so when it came
as a surprise, hidden like that until it suddenly appeared in all its
glory. The view from the bridge still takes my breath away. Even
after all these years, when I cross the bridge to go to the grocery
store, I feel my spirits lift with the rise of the road.

That first trip to Chautauqua seems like a lifetime ago. Fifteen years is a long time when it comes to family: our little kids

are now adults with budding careers, and two are married. Back then, Jeff and I were traveling with his two girls, Lisa and Kayla, and we were on an adventure. We'd seen the lake on a map, but knew nothing about it and had no plans for where we would stay. All we knew was that we were tired of spending weekends in hotel rooms if we wanted to see the girls, who lived with their mother in a tiny town near Ashtabula. That day we were road weary, too. We'd driven almost four hundred miles from our home in Delaware to pick up the girls in Ohio, and then doubled back another hour and a half to come check out this lake.

Jeff took the first exit off the bridge, and we ended up on the main street of the little village of Bemus Point. The town had a sleepy feel, and there were no hotels in sight. A post office, shops that mostly looked closed, and a couple of restaurants lined the street, which dead-ended at the lake.

"This place is interesting," Jeff said as we slowly drove up and down the quaint streets. "Different, somehow. The yards to these cottages go all the way to the water."

"It feels old-timey," I said. "I don't see any hotels, though. We better figure out if there's a place we can stay."

"I saw a real estate office on the way in," he said. "Let's go back and see if they're still open."

Jeff went in first, gave us the high sign, and the girls and I followed.

"There really aren't any hotels in this area right around here," the woman behind the desk told us. "Except for the Lenhart, and it's closed for the season. You should try the bed and breakfast over in Maple Springs. They rent rooms all year round. Just take Route 430, follow the signs toward Long Point. After you pass the Long Point sign, keep looking on your left for Guppy's Restaurant. They're open, and have good food, too. Turn toward the lake at Guppy's. Follow the road around and you'll see the bed and breakfast on the right. It's a big green house, a mansion." She handed Jeff a card. "Call me if you're looking for a summer rental."

We thanked the woman and drove back through the little town, following the road until it left the shoreline. It was almost dusk, but we could still see the lake flashing through breaks in the trees.

The turn at Guppy's led down a long, steep hill, and the road curved to the right at the lakefront. The lake was to our left; to our right were a handful of cottages, and then we spotted a large wooden sign that announced the Maple Springs Lake Side Inn. It was a two-story Dutch colonial with shutters and a slate roof, set far off the road, surrounded by a large green lawn and dormant gardens. We turned into the long driveway and parked between the back of the main house and matching two-story garage. The place looked deserted, so we got out of the car to stretch and decide what to do next.

After a couple of minutes, a small, dark-haired woman came out the back door and walked over to us. "I'm Rose," she said, offering her hand to each of us. "Can I help you with something?"

"We're looking for a room for the night, and maybe the whole weekend," Jeff said as he introduced us.

"Well, we're not open," Rose said. "We just now got back from a trip to Hawaii." She was relaxed and open, her gaze steady and guileless. We talked about Hawaii, and told her we'd just driven from Delaware.

"I could rent you an apartment in the carriage house," she said after a while. "Just the room, though. I'm not doing breakfast right now. Come on, I'll show it to you."

We followed her through a door on the main level of the garage, an old carriage house. Inside was a cozy apartment, with a living room, dining area, little kitchen, and fireplace.

"The bedroom's back here," Rose said. "There's just one, but the couch pulls out."

The girls were watching us intently to see what we'd decide.

"We'll take it," Jeff said after I nodded.

"Can we use the fireplace?" Lisa, Jeff's oldest, asked.

"Yes. There's some wood stacked outside, and a pile of newspapers over there."

"We're hungry," I said. "The real estate lady recommended Guppy's for dinner. Is that a good place?"

"It's good," Rose said. "And you should try the Bemus Point Inn for breakfast. Just go back to Bemus the way you came. It's past the real estate office a little ways, on the same side of the street. Knock on the door if you need anything; we'll be around. Sheets and blankets for the couch are in the bedroom closet. Just let me know tomorrow how long you plan to stay."

While we unloaded the car, the girls snooped around, bouncing out to report on their discoveries. They found a fully furnished kitchen, a coffee pot, and a cabinet full of playing cards and games. The apartment had a great view of the lake.

"Let's get some dinner, and tomorrow after breakfast maybe we can find a grocery store and stock up," I said. "I love it that there's a kitchen in here. Oh, Jeff, this is so much better than some crappy Holiday Inn!"

Between us, Jeff and I had four children. By this time, his girls were seven and twelve. My son was fourteen, my daughter ten. That weekend, my kids were both in Delaware with their dad. Jeff's kids lived in Ohio with their mother, but we saw them as often as we could, given the geographical separation we endured.

When we married, having all of these children was hectic, but over the years things became much more difficult. My ex-husband, formerly a pretty absent father, was threatened by my marriage and did everything he could to undermine our authority and my kids' relationships with Jeff and his children.

Jeff's ex-wife wasn't as overtly destructive. At first, we saw his children almost every month and during holidays. They would fly in Friday night, and we would fly them home Sunday evening. For a while we settled into a routine that was never easy, but was manageable. Over time, and under the influence of her new husband, Jeff's ex-wife began creating many obstacles to our spending time with his kids. It started out that she would agree to their flying to Delaware, but then she wouldn't put them on the plane. Jeff would drive to the airport in Baltimore to pick them up only to return home without them. When his frantic phone calls were finally answered, she would coolly inform him that she said they could visit, but that she never agreed to take them to the airport. Finally, she refused to send them at all, telling him that if he wanted to see them, he could come to Ohio. While Jeff was working things out through the courts, if we wanted to see them, we drove to Ohio and stayed with them in Hampton or Holiday Inns in Cleveland or Ashtabula. It was awful for us, and it put the children in a terrible spot. We could feel their agitation, but it subsided after a bit of snuggling on a couch or hotel bed. Jeff's calm presence and the warm comfort of his body made them feel safe.

Managing our blended family was the most difficult thing Jeff and I had ever done. If we had known how difficult it would be, I'm not sure that we would have had the courage to take it on. For their own reasons and employing different strategies, both of our ex-spouses were uncomfortable with our children loving us, too insecure to fully share the children. The pressures they applied to the children impeded our ability to discipline or comfort. The children were in perpetual states of unease, guarded in what they said, reluctant to relax into affection lest they betray their other parents.

The statistics for the success of second marriages with children involved are grim, and I understand why. If our crazy schedule with the children coming and going hadn't included some time when we didn't have any kids with us at all, I'm sure we wouldn't have made it. We needed that precious time alone to propel us and give us the strength to handle the rest of it. We did make it, and although we were wounded, the children bear the deepest scars.

Guppy's was packed. We gave our name to the host and stood in the tiny bar area waiting for a table. The bar was only big enough to hold about eight stools, and two four-top bar tables were jammed in under the windows. The walls were covered with college pennants and license plates from various states. Behind the bar, a mechanical Rodney Dangerfield doll occasionally blurted out his famous one-liner, "I Don't Get No Respect." A baseball cap was slung over deer antlers, with a caption that read "HOOF ARTED." Off to the left, a larger room was filled with tables covered by plastic toppers; kitschy decorations covered the walls. The mood in the place was festive and raucous. It was contagious, and soon Jeff and I were grinning like idiots.

We were seated and the waitress came over to take our orders. "The pizza's good," she said. "And make sure you save room for the ice cream bar," she told the kids.

One of the owners stopped by our table as she was making her rounds. When we told her where we were from, she welcomed us to the lake.

Later, the girls stuffed themselves at the ice cream bar. We let them go up by themselves, and they came back with bowls of ice cream covered with various syrups, sprinkles, nuts, whipped cream, and cherries. The simple act of sharing ice cream in a place of our choosing, of parenting without interference, was a balm.

The atmosphere of Guppy's, the friendliness and conviviality, felt good to us. Jeff and I had both spent time out West where the people are open and friendly. We had found the people in Delaware to be aloof and reserved. Although we had, and still have, some beloved friends there, most of the people seemed as closed in as the Delaware sky. I'm sure that part of how we felt was due to our situation. Managing our family dynamics, with all the comings and goings, the children's acting out, and the desperate need to repair when we were alone didn't do much to support an active social life, but part of it was just Delaware. We had frequented a restaurant in our neighborhood for years, but no one ever acknowledged us or acted like they'd even seen us before. Jeff and I both preferred the wildness of the West, where the human spirit is molded by the weather and horizons, and the natural surroundings give a body a sense of place in the universe. Chautauqua stirred something of this in us.

After dinner, we went back to the apartment and stayed up late playing cards and watching television. We slept like logs in our cozy room, the girls on the sleeper sofa.

The next morning we awoke to an unexpected snowfall. About eight inches had fallen, covering everything in sight, and fluffy flakes were still lightly coming down. The girls wanted to go out in it as soon as they woke, so we bundled up and trudged down to the lakefront. The scene was like a postcard, or a Currier and Ives print. The sounds were muffled, broken occasionally by quacking ducks flying by in pairs on their stubby wings, or honking geese, flying more elegantly in their noisy V patterns. They flew low and occasionally landed to fish, or perhaps to begin their search for nesting sites. We couldn't hear our footfalls, but saw our prints in the fresh snow.

We followed Rose's recommendation and had a great breakfast at the Bemus Point Inn. The girls split a giant cinnamon roll, and I had the breakfast special: sausage, eggs, and hashbrown casserole. We all ordered the "salt rise" toast. It's a local favorite, and although it looks like white toast, it has a denser texture and yeastier taste. Our bellies full, we spent most of the rest of the day poking around the lake, getting our bearings and looking for a grocery store. A two-lane highway skirts the entire north basin of the lake. We drove through little communities, passed the Chautauqua Institution, and found groceries in Mayville. We discovered the Mar-Mar liquor store and bought some wine. The old man at the counter gave us our change in funny money: two-dollar bills, Susan B. Anthony dollar coins, and Kennedy half-dollars. We passed camps and places that rented cottages and cabins, including one called "We Wan Chu" that advertised cabins and boat rentals. We drove by golf courses, one with a commanding view of the lake.

After our adventure out, we spent the rest of the afternoon watching television (the kids) or napping (us), and then went for a long walk through Maple Springs, along the lake and up and down the little residential lanes. Snow was piled high on the roofs of the cottages and hung over their eaves. The light was dim and watery, but the whiteness of the snow caused us to squint. We walked by cottages of all shapes and sizes, some painted white, blue, and gray, some more playfully bright green, coral, and yellow. Almost all the cottages had roomy porches. There were a couple of modern-looking wooden structures, but most of the houses were bungalows. The whole place had a nostalgic feel, as if it were still 1940, the sense of innocence heightened by the pristine snow.

We ate a spaghetti dinner in the apartment that evening, and Kayla even had hers with sauce, instead of her usual plain, buttered noodles. The girls were beginning to get used to my cooking, and Lisa was on the verge of becoming an adventurous eater.

Later that evening, Jeff and I put on our coats to drink a glass of wine in the little patio area out front.

"This is a neat place," Jeff said with a big grin on his face. "I know we're still in the East, but this place has more of a Midwestern or Western feel. The people are nice. I can't quite put my finger on it, but it kind of reminds me of Montana."

"It's almost like you could transplant the people from Bozeman here, and it wouldn't make any difference," I said. I leaned back into my chair, drew a deep breath, took a sip of wine, and wrapped my coat around myself more tightly. "It's not the same as Montana, but it's as beautiful. It's not as dramatic, but I like it. Look at all those stars. It's like a Western sky."

Jeff took my hand, and I couldn't remember the last time we were this relaxed or so content. We sat quietly for a long time, breathing in the clean air under that impossible sky.

Our Lake

Then close your eyes and tap your heels together three times. And think to yourself, 'There's no place like home.'

—Glinda the Good Witch

We decided to return to the lake for a family vacation at the end of Jeff's girls' five-week summer visit. My fourteen-year-old son, Matt, refused to go. He wanted to be with his friends, and was frankly outnumbered by the three little girls. Jeff reminded me of the last vacation he took with his own family. He was such a sulky little jerk that he wouldn't even walk with them in public, instead lagging behind, pretending he didn't know them. I've learned that when a teenager doesn't want to go and you make him, there is a fifty-fifty chance that he'll either settle in and have fun, or will ruin the trip for everyone, perhaps in a spectacular or embarrassing way. We see it happen with friends of ours up here now. When their children reach a certain age, trips to the lake become infrequent, miserable, or both. The kids come back around, though, after they become human again. We love having our children visit now, including my son who is a man. But there is still a broken place in my heart from missing my teenage boy.

After much preparation and incessant packing and unpacking by the three girls, my daughter and Jeff's two, we all piled into the car for the long and challenging drive. Although none of the legs of our journey were easy, we felt our spirits climb as we left the coastal plain of Delaware for the rolling hills of Pennsylvania and entered the tail end of the soft Allegheny Mountains in New York. The humidity lifted, and the sky grew bluer as we went west.

Late that afternoon we finally took the welcome turn into Maple Springs at Guppy's and pulled into the circular drive of the bed and breakfast. The sun hit the expanse of lawn at a slant, lengthening the shadows of the trees, and beyond them the lake shimmered. Rose came out to greet us and to show us our accommodations for the week. Jeff and I took the downstairs apartment we'd had before in the carriage house, and we rented the upstairs apartment for the girls. Rose led us up a steep staircase behind our apartment. We walked into a small kitchen. The living room was off to the right, facing the lake, and the girls scampered ahead to discover two bedrooms. The furnishings, like those downstairs, were comfortable and cottage-y. While the girls were claiming their chenille-covered beds, Jeff asked Rose about keys.

"I know I have some somewhere," she said. "But we don't usually lock this place. I'll look. You can lock the outside door from downstairs. That way, the girls will have to go in and out of your apartment. You'll hear any noise on the stairs, anyway."

"That'll work," Jeff said. "We have enough to keep track of without worrying about keys."

Rose laughed. "I saw a lot of suitcases. I'm glad I have boys. I serve breakfast at 8:30. I'd appreciate it if you'd let me know whether you'll be there or not. Sunday, my husband Paul takes the guests over to Bemus in the boat for breakfast at the Surf Club. The girls will like that. You'll meet him tomorrow at breakfast. And I think he's planning to take guests to the Casino on Thursday night."

"We're not gamblers," I said.

"It's not that kind of casino," Rose said with a laugh. "It's a restaurant, and they have music. Good wings and hamburgs, too."

"She said 'hamburgs,'" I said to Jeff after she left.

Jeff laughed. "I like her," he said. "Even though she's busy, she stays right with you until you're finished talking."

"You do that, too," I said. "I'm glad we decided to come back up here. It's nice to have someone who remembers us, someone who is helping us get to know the area. I know where the store is. And man, I thought this place was beautiful in the wintertime. It's like magic, now."

The girls went through the apartment, opening doors and drawers, putting their things away. We could sense them establishing ownership of the place. At twelve, Lisa had slimmed down and had that hungry look of adolescence. Sometimes a look of adult awareness would pass over her face. She liked having the role of the eldest, but the other girls put her in her place, with words or fingernails, if she took it too far and got too bossy. My daughter, Maggie, was all elbows and knees at age ten. She wore the map of Ireland across her face in freckles and had a mop of unruly auburn hair. Brief moments of adolescent self-consciousness sometimes struck, but her free, childlike spirit still dominated. Kayla was seven, a quiet, serious, and affectionate girl with thick, strawberry blond hair. The girls were thrilled to have their own place, almost as much as Jeff and I were to have ours.

The next morning, we went to the main house for breakfast. We met Paul, Rose's husband, and their boys, Pauly and Mat, who were close in age to our girls. Paul was tall, with a tight braid at the nape of his neck that disguised his long hair. He was laid back and relaxed, unlike Rose, who was perpetual motion as she cooked and served.

I noticed a few bottles of maple syrup on a small table near the door. "Is that for sale?" I asked.

"It is," Rose said. "It's local."

"We tap our trees," Paul said. "Some of our syrup is in those bottles."

"We saw some sort of tubing in the trees out back," Jeff said. "We were wondering what that was. I guess it makes sense that this place is called Maple Springs."

The sap runs in maple trees in the late winter and early spring. The peak flow comes when it freezes at night, then gets sunny and warm the next day. It's only about a four-week season, and when the trees start to bud, the taste of the syrup is ruined. An average taphole produces five to fifteen gallons of sap, but a single tree can produce forty to eighty gallons of sap in a good year. The sap must be boiled down to concentrate the sugar; it takes about ten gallons of sap to make a quart of syrup.

"How's the fishing?" Jeff asked Paul with a gleam in his eye.

Paul answered with a similar gleam, and I recognized the look only too well. "The lake's full of fish," he said. "Perch, bass, and walleye, mainly. There's muskies in there, too, but they're hard to catch." I listened patiently as they spoke the secret language of lures and bait, the habits and haunts of fish. I knew Paul wouldn't give up too much information; there is an unwritten rule that fishermen never tell exactly where the fish are biting. They joke that if they tell you, they'll have to kill you, but I'm not sure they're really joking. The fishing is serious up here.

"Can I dock a boat here?" Jeff asked. "I was thinking of renting one. I tried to call that guy Spike who advertises Boats and Worms, but he never answers."

"You can use our dock," Paul told him. "If I were you, I'd just wander down the lake and see if you can find Spike. He's usually down with his boats." He looked out the window and pointed. "Walk down the lakefront and you'll find Spike. Right by the townhouses, where Whiteside Parkway turns into Lakeside Drive."

Later that morning as I watched the girls swim off the dock, Jeff decided to try to find Spike and get a boat. He was gone for quite a while, and came back looking puzzled and slightly disturbed.

"I found Spike and got a boat for the rest of the week," he said. "But he wouldn't let me bring the boat back to keep it here." Jeff sighed. "I understand it, I guess. He wants to make sure that the boat is clean and in good shape for me to take it out the next day. He's proud of his boats. You should see this guy," he said to me. "He looks just like Popeye. He's old, but muscular. Even has a corncob pipe. When I told him where we were staying, he acted like he didn't want to rent me a boat at all, but I talked him into it. He's cranky."

The next day, Jeff got up early to fish. After breakfast, I joined the girls on the dock, reading while they swam. The lake was a little weedy, so the girls floated around on rafts to avoid the yuck. Soon they joined me on the dock trying to warm up and get suntans. The day was cool and cloudy, but we warmed up quickly when the sun peeked through.

"Wanna go for a boat ride?" Jeff pulled the boat alongside the dock. "Grab this rope and hold on," he said to the girls, and then he hopped out and tied the boat to a post.

I ran up to the apartment for some fresh towels. By the time I got back, the girls were scrunched in the boat, shivering from the cool breeze. I tossed them the towels, and they quickly wrapped up. The boat was an old aluminum fishing boat, with a couple of cross-bars for seating and an old motor mounted on the back. Jeff sat back by the motor to steer. After I got settled, off we went.

The lake was even more beautiful from the water than it was from the shore. Jeff tooled us slowly along as we watched the houses and landscape slip by. The sky was cloudy, and it was cooler on the water than it was on land. We floated by the cottages in Maple Springs with their green lawns and drifted in front of Midway, the old amusement park. From the water we could see a long dock, a swimming beach, and a large, wooden building with MIDWAY painted across the black roof in white letters. The water was gray and a little choppy. Jeff said it was perfectly calm when he went out that morning, but he didn't have much luck fishing.

As we continued down the shoreline, we saw the large grounds of big camps and church retreats, then clusters of cottages, occasionally broken up by larger houses with vast lawns. There were thickly wooded areas in places, but otherwise the lawns went all the way down to the water. When the sun came out, it was dazzling. The contrast of the grays, blues, and greens with the soft, wooded hills behind took my breath away.

"There's something about this place I can't quite put my finger on," I said. "It feels . . . well . . . restorative." I felt the sun warm my back as the wind ruffled my hair. "I don't think I've ever said that before about a place, or felt it. Not like this."

Jeff took in the shoreline, inhaled deeply, and then struck out across the lake. On the far shore, cottages dotted the shoreline in clusters, just like on our side. Beyond that, the landscape rose into wooded hills until it met the sky.

"That's the bell tower for the Chautauqua Institution," Jeff said, pointing north. I made out a tall brick structure with a white roof, a clock face angled toward the lake.

"I thought I heard a clock chime this morning," I said. "We'll have to drive over there sometime. We really should go explore."

"We're freezing!" Lisa yelled. I looked back, and the girls were huddled in their towels on the bottom of the boat. Only their little heads were visible. In my reverie, I'd forgotten about them entirely.

I glanced at Jeff, and as he turned the boat around to head back, he revved the motor and we sped up. It was a bumpy ride, especially when we'd hit a big wave or a wake from another boat. The bumps jarred my teeth.

"Slow down!" I yelled, grabbing the side of the boat with one hand and my chest with the other.

He complied with a grin, and soon we pulled in alongside the dock.

"You wouldn't like going fast, either, if you had boobs," I laughed as the girls scrambled out and ran to the apartment for warm showers. I cautiously climbed out, feeling a little wobbly and windblown, and then Jeff headed back down the lake to return the boat to Spike.

Rose and Paul were sitting on their patio and waved me over. "Come have a glass of wine with us," Rose said. "You look like you could use one. It's choppy out there. Did Jeff have any luck fishing?"

"He said he just caught some little sunnies," I said. "And what's with that Spike guy? Jeff said he was really cranky, and he won't let us have the boat down here."

Rose laughed. "Spike's cantankerous. He used to own a hotel down on the lake. He sold it, then they tore it down. But he still acts like he owns the lakefront. He's really just a squatter, and the neighbors bitch all the time about his boat business. He's really not supposed to do that. We have to have something to bitch about, though, so we don't get out of practice."

"The politics are thick in Maple Springs," Paul said. "Spike's suspicious of people he doesn't know, and he doesn't like the people at this end of town. I'm surprised he rented Jeff a boat at all, once he found out he was staying here. We own our lakefront, but most of the waterfront is community property, owned by the Whiteside Allotment. New people move in and think they can put their docks up anywhere they want, but they can't. Some guy tried to put a dock up on our property not too long ago. I ran him off. The realtors don't help—they tell everybody they have lake rights, which technically they do if they're on this side of Chautauqua Avenue. But just because you have lake rights doesn't mean you can put a dock in."

We heard, and then saw, an old pickup truck, red and rusted, pull into the driveway. Jeff was in the passenger seat, and an old man was at the wheel.

Rose's jaw dropped. "I don't believe it. That's Spike!"

Spike gave our group a little wave. We could see him jabbering through the windshield. I knew Spike was doing most of the talking, since Jeff is a quiet person. He's a good listener, though, and it was another half-hour before he got out of the truck.

"Man, that guy can talk," Jeff said. "I didn't think I'd ever get out of that truck. He knows a lot about fishing on this lake, though."

"Oh, yeah," said Paul. "Spike will talk your ear off. You should consider yourself privileged that he's talking to you at all. He's in the tourist business, but it usually takes him a while to warm up." Paul shook his head. "I can't believe he gave you a ride back here. I thought I'd seen everything by now, but I never thought I'd see that."

"Next time we come, I might try to find a different boat rental place," Jeff said. "That guy's a character, but I'd really like a boat I could keep here. Come and go on my own schedule."

"There's a guy in Bemus that rents fishing boats," Paul said. "Or you could try We Wan Chu, across the lake. First dibs go to people who are staying in their cabins, though."

The next morning, after Jeff returned from fishing, we took the girls to Midway. Earlier in the week, they spent hours counting out and dividing the change that Jeff had brought. Throughout the year, he tossed his change into a coffee can and, as in previous years, this was the girls' vacation spending money. They ended up with a pretty good haul of almost sixty dollars each, and it was burning a hole in their pockets.

We walked the few blocks from the bed and breakfast to the end of Chautauqua Avenue and entered a gate through a high chain-link fence that enclosed Midway's parking lot on the side facing the residential area of Maple Springs. The gate provides no security since the fence dead-ends on either side, but it does prevent people from driving in through that entrance if it's locked. For generations, teenagers have been hanging out at Midway after hours. In addition to an antique carousel, old photo booths, a roller rink, and ancient arcade games, Midway is filled with first kisses, stolen kisses, teenage hormones, and true love.

The park was large, with a green lawn and gardens filled with hydrangeas, impatiens, and black-eyed Susans. Hanging baskets and huge containers of petunias lined the walkways. Picnic tables dotted the grassy areas, and there were a number of covered pavilions for picnics, reunions, and parties near a small swimming beach.

The gift shop was filled with tchotchkes devoted to Chautauqua Lake and Midway: T-shirts, hats, keychains, pencils, and insulated coffee cups. There were stuffed animals, toys, cheap jewelry, and postcards. The walls were covered with old photographs: steamships unloading passengers dressed in funny, old-fashioned clothing onto Midway's huge old dock; swimmers clad in striped onesies, showing nothing but heads, arms, and knobby knees; women in long skirts carrying parasols; pictures of Lucille Ball. Several photographs showed pairs of smiling skaters, men and women in clothes long out of fashion. The women had hairdos where the outlines of the brush rollers and bobby pins were visible. Some of the photographs had notes posted underneath that indicated the couples' names, the dates they met at the roller rink, and when they married.

I called the girls to come have their fortunes told by Princess Doraldina, a mechanical Gypsy seated in an old wooden cabinet. She was draped in silk and jewels; Tarot cards were spread out in front of her hands.

Lisa inserted a quarter into the retrofitted slot marked for nickels, and Princess Doraldina came to life. Suddenly illuminated, she moved her hand back and forth across the cards. She creaked as we watched her eyes move, her head nod, and her chest lift and fall with each robotic breath. The other girls looked on, their eyes as big as saucers, until a paper fortune fell through a slot into a brass receptacle. The card was marked with arcane symbols and mysterious runes. The fortune itself was baffling: "*You have gotten the big card. This means you will gain something great in the near future. All men's gains are the fruit of venturing . . .*" We all remained transfixed and a little spooked as everyone took her turn. We'd seen *Big*, the Tom Hanks movie where he turns into a 12-year-old adult by making a wish on the same sort of contraption, and I could tell the girls were being careful about what they wished for, just in case.

Those early years are mostly a jumbled blur, but some images of our lake visits at the bed and breakfast remain vivid in my mind. Lisa standing barefoot on the patio of our apartment at the bed and breakfast in a white, strapless dress. Her skin was porcelain. She shielded her eyes from the sun and looked like an angel. I'd found the dress at an antique store for seven dollars, and she wore it to her first dance. The kids playing "pudgy bunny" around the fire pit on the lakefront at night, stuffing their mouths with marshmallows while they tried to say the words: *pudgy bunny, pudgy bunny, pudgy bunny.* Sparky the dog gobbled up whatever fell out of their mouths. Maggie racing around the circular driveway of the bed and breakfast in an old Midway go-cart, hair flying. Girls flopping gracelessly onto swimming rafts from the dock to avoid the weeds, and then flinging weeds at each other when they got over their squeamishness. Jeff putting countless worms on hooks, and pulling fish off when they were caught. Everyone felt sorry for the fish but Maggie, who baited her own hooks, pulled off her own fish, and slapped them back into the lake with a big splash.

Kayla's bloody foot, sliced open when she heaved herself onto a rock wall for pictures. One picture shows her smiling, the next captures her scream.

Our love for the lake began on our first trip, and deepened as we continued to visit. Over the next couple of years, we spent more and more time there, getting familiar with the rhythms and offerings of the place. We became regulars at the bed and breakfast, staying in the carriage house where we had more privacy and our own kitchen. Jeff, and sometimes, when I could get away, Jeff, Maggie, and I, could look forward to spending time in this comfortable place, instead of those awful hotel rooms in Ohio. The place provided a haven, solace for our fractured family. Although we were only visitors, the lake was growing on us. We felt tethered by Delaware's milky skies and flat horizons. The light at the lake was brighter, more luminous, the landscape more dramatic, and we felt like we could breathe. The lake felt like possibility.

As soon as we found Chautauqua Lake, Jeff and I had fantasies about getting our own place up there. The idea of owning our own lake place was both tantalizing and frightening. It was a big commitment, but we lived modestly in Delaware and figured that if we got a good enough deal, I could pay the mortgage with my earnings while Jeff kept the rest of our boat floating with his. And the prices were very reasonable, especially compared to the beach house prices we'd seen in Delaware. We would likely spend a lot of time at the lake over the next few years because of his children, and if we got our own place, at least we'd have something to show for it, something tangible.

We watched the *Homes* magazines and occasionally went to open houses. We rode around with realtors more than once, but didn't find anything to our liking that was in our price range.

We'd frankly been spoiled by Maple Springs. It felt more like a community to us instead of just a cluster of houses on the lake. Houses turn over slowly there, so we looked in other areas. We made a low-ball offer on a cottage in Point Chautauqua, and were immediately outbid by a flurry of other prospective buyers, secretly relieved we didn't get it. A cottage came open in Maple Springs. It had potential but needed a lot of work, and the yard was too small to even hold a picnic table. I asked the realtor to let us know if anything else came open in Maple Springs, and he eventually contacted me about a two-bedroom townhouse. We were not enthusiastic. Two bedrooms was too small.

The next weekend, I was home in Delaware while Jeff was at the lake with his girls. The phone rang, and it was Jeff.

"I looked at that townhouse," he said. "In Maple Springs. It's only two bedrooms, but it's right on the lake."

"I'm not sure where it is," I said. "Is that the place we walk by? Where the road curves?"

"Yeah," he said. "Where I rented the boats from Spike that time. We've seen people sitting on the lakefront down there, remember? I think it might work. It's only got the two bedrooms, but it feels like a nice hotel suite or something. No crud factor, like so many of those other places we've seen. It has a little kitchen, and a fireplace in the living room."

"What's the bathroom like?" I asked.

"Just a sec," Jeff said. "Let me pull over. I'll call you right back."

The break was long enough for me to pour another cup of coffee and take a few deep breaths. Regardless of how things looked on paper, making any kind of purchase beyond the usual groceries or junk finds made me nervous. Jeff had to write the checks for appliances or any other big-ticket items, even if the money came out of my own checking account, from my own earnings.

"Hey," I said when he called back. "Just here getting a grip on myself."

"The bedrooms are upstairs. We could make one of the bedrooms work for the girls if we had two sets of bunk beds. The view is great," Jeff said. "There's a full bathroom upstairs, too, and another little bathroom downstairs. We could put Matt on a couch if he ever decides to join us up there. I think we could make it comfortable."

"Oh, geez," I said. "I'm kind of scared, but if you think so, I think we should go ahead and make an offer. I can't believe I'm saying yes to a place I've never seen. But I trust your instincts. If you think it will work, I think we should do it."

We made an offer, and it was accepted. We'd grown to love the lake and the community that surrounded it. Buying a place would mean that we'd be part of that community, instead of just observers. What we couldn't get people to understand was that this wouldn't simply be a vacation place for us, it would be *our* place. A safe place to bring the children; a neutral place where we could rest and relax; a place that lifted our spirits and felt like home.

Boats

There is NOTHING—absolutely nothing—half so much worth doing as simply messing about in boats.

—Kenneth Grahame *(The Wind in the Willows)*

The boat was sitting on a trailer in our driveway. It was filthy, covered by a blue tarp that was ripped and mostly blown off by the wind. An elastic band held its remnants over the bow. As I headed over to take a closer look, Jeff came out of the house. He had a big grin on his face but looked a little sheepish. I knew he was excited about it, and anxious about my reaction.

He'd been talking about this boat for weeks. It belonged to his dad, who said Jeff could have it if he could get it from Texas to Delaware. Jeff's parents lived in a retirement community on Falcon Lake near Zapata, Texas, on the Mexican border. Billed as resort living, it was really a trailer park: resort living for retired blue-collar workers. I'd been down once and had been fascinated by the lifestyle. The old people rode around on golf carts visiting one another, mostly talking about their ailments or engaging in idle gossip. Other times they exchanged medications. They could get the drugs cheaply in Mexico, without a prescription, and coordinated their orders. The old desperados would cross over into a run-down Mexican border town to buy vanilla, liquor, and tchotchkes and load up on drugs.

The state of Texas diverted water from the Rio Grande to California and then a drought struck, so by the time I visited, Falcon Lake had dried up. Instead of fishing, all the old people perched around the rim of the dry lake and bitched about the "resort" owner, who spent his time moving dirt around with a backhoe at the bottom of what was now a big hole. To what end was anybody's guess.

During a break in his company's construction schedule, Jeff had been able to free up a couple of his traveling superintendents, Marshall and Budweiser Dave, to haul the boat. These guys traveled from job to job, building out retail stores in malls all over the country. They'd finished a job in Texas, and then driven up to Delaware to deposit the boat.

"This is a classic," Jeff said as I peered in over the tarp to look at the interior. "It runs, but probably needs a new motor, and I'm going to replace the seats and the carpet."

The boat was flesh-colored fiberglass, its hull painted with faded red and darker tan stripes. The carpet, which ran across the floor and up the sides, was filthy, and stuffing was coming out of the rips in the tan captain's chair that sat unevenly behind the steering wheel. The other seats were ripped, too. The interior was open, with an old motor mounted at the rear. A removable Plexiglas panel in the middle of the windshield, designed for climbing onto the bow, was cracked and chipped.

"How big is this thing?" I asked.

"It's an eighteen-foot Larson," Jeff said. "1963. It's a classic."

"I was just thinking it looks like a classic," I said. I wasn't really trying to be sarcastic, but nothing about the boat conjured up the word *classic* for me. I noticed what looked like a network of fishing line strung across the boat in several places. "What's this?"

"My dad made a homemade alarm," Jeff said. "Half of Falcon Lake is in Mexico. Dad said Mexican thieves would come over at night in boats to steal batteries and fishpoles and stuff. He rigged this so if the fishing line was disturbed, an alarm would go off." Jeff laughed. "I guess then he was going to jump in the golf cart and beat the thieves over the head with his oxygen tank."

"Hmmmm," I said. "So it's not just a classic, it's a well-protected classic."

"Well, what do you think?" Jeff asked. He was still nervous about what my reaction would be.

"I was just thinking that you've lost your fucking mind," I said. "And wondering what could possibly make you think it was worth it to haul this piece of shit up from Texas."

By this time I was laughing, and then we were both laughing.

Jeff worked furiously over the next few weeks to get the boat ready to have it in the water at Chautauqua by the time the docks went in. He ripped up the carpet and patched a big hole in the floor, which explained why the captain's chair was leaning so precariously. He covered the plywood deck with new carpet, installed six new red seats, replaced the broken Plexiglas, and got a reconditioned motor that worked. I didn't ask what any of this cost, but after considerable experience I've learned that there is no such thing as a free boat.

Years later I met Marshall and Budweiser Dave in person, at one of Jeff's company meetings. Marshall was smaller than I'd imagined him, and wiry, with a bald head and beaky nose. Budweiser

Dave looked like his name implied, only worse. During dinner, Marshall entertained everyone with stories and one-liners.

"How's your mother-in-law, Beth?" he asked.

"She's getting battier all the time, but her health is good," I replied, glancing at Jeff.

"Well, you tell her I said to quit running around outside nek-kid, making the neighbors go blind. That's what I tell my mother-in-law." He laughed and took a swig of beer. "And my wife, now she wants a pool boy. We don't even have a pool!"

Somehow we got on the subject of the boat. Turns out that while they were hauling it, the police had stopped Marshall and Budweiser Dave, twice. Even though the paperwork was all in order, both times they were subjected to searches by drug-sniffing dogs. Apparently the cops didn't understand why anyone would haul that piece of shit from Texas to Delaware either.

~

We had closed on the townhouse long distance the previous winter, and during the spring Jeff and I had made a couple of trips to start moving in. I fell in love with the place immediately. It was compact, clean, and laid out to be functional, even though it was small. The living space was extended by porches on either side: a porch with patio off the parking lot, and a sitting porch that faced the lake. Opening the blinds on the sliding glass door brought the lakefront into the living room.

When we heard the docks were installed, we made a proper trip up to launch the boat. The drive seemed especially long, hauling the boat behind the big truck. Only Maggie was with us that day, sleeping most of the way, snuggled into the back seat with blankets and pillows.

When we got to the townhouse, Jeff pulled the boat behind the shed and got out to unhitch the trailer. While he was messing with the boat, Maggie and I lugged our suitcases inside.

"Wow, this place is cool!" she said as I showed her the kitchen and the tiny downstairs bathroom. We walked through the living room, and I raised the blinds on the sliding door. The sun was beginning its slow afternoon arc downward, and came streaming into the room. The lake was sparkling as the sunlight bounced off the wavelets.

I left her to explore and unpack. Jeff had made no progress unhitching the boat, but was standing by it, talking with an old man. I recognized Spike immediately and walked over to join them.

"Weeeell, hello there," the old man said, offering his hand. "I'm Spike. Welcome to the neighborhood. Anything you need to know about the lake, or about Maple Springs, you just ask me. I'm kind of like the mayor around here. Yup, kind of like the mayor."

He turned back toward Jeff. "This is a nice boat you've got here. When you going to put it in? You don't see many boats like this anymore. No, you sure don't."

Spike talked and we listened. Occasionally Jeff would ask a question and Spike would be off again. Spike *did* look like Popeye. He wasn't tall, but he was big, with broad, sloping shoulders and tanned, muscular arms. His face was lined and tan, and he wore a cap to cover his bald head. Under loose shorts, his legs were thick and bowed. He wore boat shoes, with no socks. He was even more colorful in person than he'd seemed when I saw him through his truck window the summer that Jeff rented one of his boats.

"Hey, that's a great boat you've got there." I turned and saw a nice-looking older man walking toward us from the townhouses. Wearing a pressed polo shirt and shorts, he nodded a greeting to Spike and extended his hand toward Jeff. "I'm Butch Falkner. You must be Jeff. Pleased to finally meet you." The Falkner's lived two doors down from us, in Unit 2. He turned to me and extended his hand again. "Beth, isn't it?" he asked. "Welcome to Maple Springs."

"We've been here since the place was built," Butch said. "In 1988. We stay here during the summer, but spend the winters in Florida. Before they built the townhouses, this place was a hotel, owned by Mr. Spike Kelderhouse here."

"Yup," Spike said proudly. "Ran the hotel, and had a charter fishing business. I grew up here on this lake. Bought my first boat when I was eighteen, and I've been a boat man ever since."

As we were chatting, a white van pulled into the parking lot and stopped beside us. The driver rolled down his window.

"Hey, Mr. Kelderhouse. Mr. Falkner. Beautiful day on the lake, isn't it?"

"Always is," said Butch. "Mike, have you met your new neighbors?"

The van's occupants tumbled out. Linda O'Connor was pretty, with cornflower blue eyes and a broad, open face with dimples that showed when she smiled. She was holding Colleen, a toddler, in her arms. Kathryn, the older girl, clung shyly to her mother's legs.

"I didn't think we'd ever get here," Linda said, breathlessly. "Girls, tell Mr. Spike that we're ready to fish. We brought our fishing poles, now all we need are some worms."

After he parked the van, Mike walked over to join the group. Like Linda, he was warm and energetic.

"I've left a kid in the house," I said, turning to go back inside.

"I hope you can join us out front for happy hour," Butch said. "You'll want to meet my wife, Margie. Come on over about five. We'll either be on our porch or down by the lake."

"I'm going in, too," Linda said. "I've got a lot of unpacking to do." She pronounced it "unpecking," with a Buffalo accent.

By the time I finished unloading and got to our porch, Linda and her kids were already on the dock fishing. Linda was standing with her arms akimbo, hands covered with green dishwashing gloves. I sat down next to Maggie to take in the view.

The townhouses sit on a big lawn right on the lakefront. The lawn is full of trees, with a couple of towering old maples, tall beeches, and smaller trees, newly planted. There is plenty of open area, big enough for badminton or playing ball, and the view of the lake is mostly unobstructed. The shoreline is crowded with docks. Ours was the biggest, with enough boatlifts for our six units. A pontoon boat was tied up along one side. The pontoon belonged to Butch and Marge, and they often had their happy hour on it. Pontoon boats are good for large groups, and for older people who can't manage jumping into or climbing out of other kinds of boats.

A mishmash of brightly painted metal chairs sat in rows or clustered in groups of three or four near the shore, along with a wooden glider and two wooden Adirondack chairs. Rickety, brightly painted side tables were placed strategically among the chairs.

Rowboats, sailboats, and kayaks were pulled up on the sandy shore between the docks. I would later learn that the docks belonged to the Cummiskeys, the Kelderhouses, the Arvidsons, and the Whitbecks. The dock belonging to the Arvidsons had a small sign in front that read "Arvidson's Landing."

Spike's fleet of aluminum fishing boats, about ten in all, was pulled up on the shore where the road curves. A couple more were tied up to the Kelderhouse dock. Most of the docks had two or more boats in boatlifts, and a few boats were tied up to buoys in the water. Instead of walking out onto a dock to get into a boat, these boaters would row a skiff out to the buoy and transfer to the motorboat from there. History, friendship, and a lot of negotiation went into who owned the docks and who shared the docks. Because the lake freezes hard in the winter, docks and boatlifts are taken out in the fall and put back in during spring. Docks going in, docks coming out, where the dock sections were stacked, dock placement, and dock configuration were a source of constant discussion, negotiation, and frequent bitching.

Maggie and I walked toward the dock to join the O'Connors. As we drew closer, we heard a funny noise, one I didn't recognize. A two-stroke breathy heave, shoo, choo, shoo, choo.

"Here comes the Belle!" Kathryn O'Connor cried. We turned and saw a double-decker boat with a paddlewheel and ornate decking coming down the lake toward us. Every little while, steam shot out and floated white against the blue sky.

"That's the Chautauqua Belle," Linda said. "It's a replica of an old paddlewheel steamship, like they used to have on the lake." She picked a worm up out of a Styrofoam container with her gloved hand, shaking it off before she put it on a hook. "You can still see the concrete abutments for the dock where the steamers came into Maple Springs, right over there by the swimming beach."

"This is Maggie," I said as I introduced my daughter.

"I'd shake your hand, but my gloves are kind of yukky," she said, laughing. "This is the only way I'll put worms on their hooks.

That's Kathryn," she said, indicating the older girl. "She's seven. Colleen is two. Almost three, aren't you, Colleeny?"

Kathryn was waving frantically at the Belle. Maggie joined in, and soon we heard the whistle, deep and long, whooooooooooooo, whooooooooooo, in a harmonic minor key. We stood on the dock for a long time, waving like idiots and watching the boat float by, passengers waving back.

~

Early the next morning, Jeff decided to get his boat in the water and on the lift, where he could make the minor adjustments needed to have it ready for the season. Just as I settled onto the porch with my coffee, I heard the rumble of the big truck and watched it pull around the lakefront. Spike was driving, with the boat behind on the trailer.

Jeff got out of the passenger side to direct Spike into the water. Once the boat was loosely floating on the trailer, Jeff walked into the water, climbed in, and started it. He slowly backed around, and then sped down the lake out of my sight while Spike pulled the truck and trailer out of the water. I watched as Jeff came back into view. Spike ran out to the end of the dock and barked advice while Jeff slowly pulled into the lift. The two men talked for a minute, and then Jeff crossed the lawn to where I waited on the porch. His shorts were wet almost to the waist, but he looked peaceful and satisfied.

That image of Jeff pulling slowly toward the dock that first time is still with me. Not because it was particularly memorable, but because I've seen the image so many times since: Jeff in a

T-shirt pulled tight over his broad shoulders, a Panama hat shading his tanned face, sitting straight as an arrow behind the steering wheel while the boat cuts smoothly through the water. As soon as he's near enough for me to see, I notice his face is radiant. It's the same image whether the sun shines or is covered by clouds, whether the fish are biting or after a long stretch of bad luck. When Jeff exits the boat, he's somehow larger, more complete. The lines of Jeff seem slightly more in focus. He's clearer. Something in him is restored.

~

On Chautauqua Lake, as on any lake, boats provide not only entertainment and a means to fish, they provide a backdrop to the life and culture of the entire community. Boat doings are part of the daily conversation during the season: who bought one, who sold one, whose is broken, whose is fixed, who got towed, who saved them, whose is accumulating a disproportionate amount of shit from the gulls and geese, who has designed a clever system for repelling the birds. Getting boats ready for the summer occupies the guys all spring; winterizing them, pulling them from the lake onto trailers, and figuring out storage occupies the guys well into the fall. Of course some women own their own boats, and many drive them, but the incessant messing with them seems to be a guy thing.

Boats provide considerable lakefront entertainment, for both passengers and those of us who might be observing from shore. We've seen people catch lunkers right off our dock, and watched countless children squeal with delight as they reel in tiny sunfish. Boats fly by pulling kids in tubes, or people on skis, and we've taken our share of passengers tubing and skiing as well. Jeff loves to send a cocky kid flying off the tube almost as much as he loves pulling a kid up on skis for his or her first time.

One morning in June, Jeff and I were standing on the lakefront chatting with our neighbor, Mike O'Connor. As we talked, George Whitbeck waved as he headed for his boat with his son and little grandson. The grandson was three years old at the time. They were carrying nets, poles, and tackle boxes. We continued our chat as they readied their boat and pulled around in front of the dock to troll over to George's favorite fishing spot on down the lake toward Sunset Bay. The kid hollered out, "Daddy, I'm stuck!" We heard George roar with laughter, and saw them grabbing nets, both men laughing. They pulled back into their dock and tumbled out of the boat. The boy had caught a huge muskellunge with his little Tigger fishing pole purchased from Walmart. Soon the lakefront was full of people watching and laughing. Sandra Whitbeck came running down from her house with a camera and snapped several pictures of the poor kid, scared out of his mind, standing next to a very toothy fish that was bigger than he was, bawling his head off. The story with photo appeared in the *Post-Journal* later in the week.

Another time we awoke to a big commotion. By the time we got outside, emergency vehicles and a large crowd had gathered along the lakefront road. A young man, visiting a neighbor, had gone out early to fish, and when he reached back to get some worms, his hands left the steering wheel, the boat turned sharply, and he was tossed overboard. By the time we got there, the kid had been rescued by another fisherman, but the boat was still racing in circles, driverless.

All morning long, firefighters and rescue workers put on wetsuits, took off wetsuits, and exchanged ideas for stopping the boat.

They took a boat out to see if someone could jump into the rogue boat, but that didn't work out, and then somebody decided to go back to the fire hall to get a volleyball net. Once the net arrived, they piled into a boat and tried to get close to the driverless boat.

"What are they going to do?" I asked one of the firefighters.

"They're going to try to lasso the prop," he said.

In the end, although we were greatly entertained, their efforts failed. We watched the boat go round and round all day until it finally ran out of gas. Sometimes there is nothing to do but let things run their course.

During our time of loss, when we had those moments that were too sad for tears, or when we were too filled with grief to muster the strength to tackle the next project, our old boat offered solace. Lugging our exhausted selves and a six-pack of beer to the dock, we lowered the lift and adjusted our loads for a ride. On the water, the horizon pulled us outside ourselves as the wind lifted our burdens. We brought our fractured lives to the boat and the water helped us float. For a while, at least, we were buoyant.

Many complex factors go into the boating hierarchy here at Chautauqua. I imagine that in places like Southern California or Martha's Vineyard, the focus is on who has the biggest or most expensive yacht, but here things are more subtle, although it depends on who is doing the judging.

Even though there are sailboats on the lake, most of us in Maple Springs have motorboats. The sailboat culture is entirely outside my frame of reference. Sailing is an avocation of the well-to-do; girls like me, from the wrong side of the tracks, generally do not sail.

Among the motorboats and their owners, the first major division is between those who use their boats solely for recreation and those who use their boats primarily for fishing. The recreational boaters are more likely to have bigger, more expensive, and more comfortable boats, but are less likely to know anything about them or to do their own work on them. They take them out to sun or swim, ski or tube, and to socialize, either in the boat or at one of the many lakefront bars or restaurants.

Fishing boats are prized more for their functionality than their accoutrements. While the fishermen may also use their boats to tour the lake, pull skiers, or socialize, their boats' value lies in the ease with which they can cast, move around to net a fish, maneuver into fishing spots, and comfortably stow tackleboxes, fishpoles, nets, and coolers of beer. Boaters who primarily fish are more likely to fix their own boats. They have a more intimate knowledge of their boats, and of the lake itself. They know the contours of the shoreline, the inlets and rivulets, the weedy areas, and the deep holes. They know the lake in sunshine and in shadow, in the misty dawn and the calm at dusk. They know the winds, the storm patterns, and the delicate changes of season.

Among real fishermen, there is a sense of regard for old boats. Initially, the design, the lines, or the manufacturer will be admired, but something else is operating underneath. There is respect for the unseen and unknown places an old boat has been, unspoken acknowledgment of the care that has been bestowed upon it, and an almost spiritual accounting of the fish that have been hauled in over the hull.

Jeff's dad is gone now. The water has returned to Falcon Lake, and the Mexican pirates are back to thieving. We still have the old boat. It's sitting on the trailer in the back yard of our new house. When something breaks, we fix it. We've repaired it so many times, I tease Jeff that the only original thing left is the glove box. It suits us.

Cowgirl's Prayer

Courage is being scared to death . . . and saddling up anyway.

—John Wayne

It was a beautiful evening, warm and clear. The wind, often brisk in the afternoon, had settled down for the night. Jeff and I decided to take the boat to the Chautauqua Institution; we had tickets to see Emmylou Harris.

During the summers, in addition to the more highbrow stuff, the Institution holds "Amphitheater Specials" which include popular music and other acts. We've seen some great concerts there, including The Doobie Brothers, Jethro Tull, Elvis Costello, The Chenille Sisters, and Lyle Lovett and His Large Band. Bill Cosby gave a wonderful, intimate performance there, and Garrison Keillor was there not long ago, telling masterfully woven stories and singing old hymns that sounded almost primeval in the spare, churchlike atmosphere of the amphitheater. Because he suspected there might be a large number of Unitarians in the audience, he chose hymns that didn't directly mention Jesus, instead involving the audience in a haunting rendition of *We Shall Overcome* that echoed off the rafters and floated out over the lake. He gave out a potato salad recipe, too, but mine is better because I omit the celery and add vermouth. I agree with his point, though: potato salad must be homemade or there's simply not enough love in it.

Our friend Scott, who grew up in Maple Springs, told a story about seeing Judy Collins at the Institution over thirty years ago, when Scott was in his early twenties. He said her voice sounded spectacular in the amphitheater, but the way she closed that show still haunts him. After her last song with the band, she sang an *a cappella* version of *Amazing Grace*, climbing down from the stage to walk among the people before she made her way backstage, still softly singing. Scott said there was no applause, and that you could hear a pin drop as the audience made their way out of the auditorium. People had tears streaming down their faces, or were too stunned to cry, the moment was so sacred and so deep.

In preparation for Emmylou, I packed a picnic of cold chicken, potato salad, fruit, and bread, and stuck some bottles of beer and an opener into the cooler. I make Julia Child's potato salad, salting the hot, cooked potatoes and letting them absorb some vermouth before I add a tiny bit of mustard and mayonnaise, sometimes herbs, depending on my mood and what I have on hand. A towel and a couple of sweatshirts went into a backpack. Even on warm nights in July, it can be cool on the water.

The boat ride was lovely. We hugged the shore past Midway, then headed across the lake. Even though we can see the Institution from our dock, both time and distance seem to stretch out on the water. We pushed the boat up to a pretty good speed, but the opposite shore seemed to stay far away until we were right up on it.

There is a large community dock at the Institution where residents park their boats, and if there's space, visitors can park there for events. As we neared it, we were waved over by a young man who pointed out a vacant spot and helped us tie up. Jeff slipped him five dollars. There is no charge to park, but tipping is the custom for anyone who wants his boat to be remembered and acknowledged the next time.

We picnicked in the boat, watching other concert-goers pull into their slips and walk up the long dock toward the shore.

We'd seen Emmylou Harris before, in Philadelphia, when she was on her *Wrecking Ball* tour.

"I liked the way she experimented with different sounds on *Wrecking Ball*," Jeff said. "I thought that album was great."

"I liked it too," I said. "But I hope she plays some of the old stuff tonight."

We loved her haunting voice, sometimes breathy, often strong and melodic. When her voice breaks occasionally, whether by design or accident, it adds to the plaintiveness of her singing.

"Does Emmylou Harris write her own songs?" I asked.

"Some of them," Jeff said.

"Did she write 'Queen of the Silver Dollar'?"

He shook his head. "Nope. Shel Silverstein did."

"Okay, another example of how I know you're an idiot savant." I first called him an idiot savant when he rattled off all of the songs from the *Let it Bleed* album—in order—after I asked him a question about a song, and it's become a permanent joke in our repertoire of stupid marital jokes. One of the reasons he fell in love with me, Jeff says, is that I get the joke, and somehow it's the eighth-grade-boy jokes that tickle me the most.

We laughed at my comment, but it's eerie what Jeff sometimes knows about music. Although he has no musical rhythm, a terrible singing voice, and can't dance, he is an audiophile. Music is a big part of our lives. We attend several concerts a year, and we always have something playing in the foreground or background, depending on our moods. Our tastes run toward the eclectic; we listen to everything except hip-hop and rap, and our favorite artists (besides the Rolling Stones), are probably those singer/songwriters who don't fit comfortably in a specific genre. Emmylou Harris is in this category, and we've followed her as she moved from her roots with Gram Parsons through country, folk, bluegrass, rock, and even a little bit of jazz. She is a prolific solo artist and has backed up scores of other musicians, adding a layer of richness and depth that they could never achieve on their own.

We were looking forward to this concert, but as we sat in the boat we could feel a different undercurrent swirling around us. Although neither of us had mentioned it, both of us were remembering how Emmylou Harris played nonstop in almost a never-ending loop those days and nights we fell in love years ago.

Jeff and I had been only friendly acquaintances in Montana during the 1970s, where he was beginning a career in construction and I was barely in my twenties, finishing school and trying to find myself after a bad and chaotic childhood. We ran with the same gang and hung out at Jeff's dilapidated house in Bozeman. He and two friends rented it for a hundred dollars a month, utilities included. The bathroom was so small that I had to leave the door open and hang my legs out into the kitchen to sit on the toilet.

Later, Jeff told me that if he went to bed with a glass of water on his nightstand, it would be frozen solid by morning. I lived in a similarly dilapidated house. My room was actually a pantry that contained a narrow bed, a hot water heater, and a built-in bank of doors and drawers. Once, during a particularly cold spell, the pipes burst, freezing my clothes solidly in the drawers. I'd gone to Montana with the idea of going back to school, but I really went because I had no place else to go. Like Harry Potter, I slept in my pantry, living on bean burritos and drinking Burgie beer until I found enough solid ground to plant my feet in the university and finish a bachelor's degree.

Jeff and I eventually married other people. He married a friend of mine, and I married someone I'd met at the university. We went to each others' weddings and we both married the wrong people. Damaged women have a tendency to marry people who are exactly and specifically wrong for them. Though unaware, they choose someone who is like the person who created the most pain in their childhoods, and then engage in an awful dance to try to achieve a different relational outcome. The unconscious desperately wants to resolve that old pain, to work it out so it's all better. Although I didn't know it then, that's exactly what I did, not realizing that the past cannot be repaired. Having the distraction of children made the marriage tolerable for a while, but the inevitable divorce was only deferred.

Jeff is not damaged. He married the wrong person out of love and hopeful good spirit, although there was possibly a lack of discernment caused by youth.

Over the years, Jeff and I kept in loose touch, mainly through Christmas cards. I followed my ex-husband to his job in Delaware, while Jeff and his wife eventually headed for Denver when the Montana economy collapsed in the 1980s. The first time we spoke after we'd each left Montana was in the early 1990s, when Jeff planned a trip east to attend a high school reunion in upstate New York. I was divorced by then; Jeff and his high school chum stopped by my little house in Delaware, and we went to dinner with my two children. I remember after he left thinking that Jeff had turned into a nice man. That was it.

The following year, Jeff called to invite me to a surprise party he was having for his wife, who was pressuring him into moving to Ohio, where her family lived. Although she and I had lost our close connection over the years, I believe he hoped I could talk her out of it, perhaps by sharing with her the difficulties that life as a single parent brings. I went to the party, and it was nice to see some old Montana friends. But after a conversation I'd had with his wife and oldest daughter, I pulled him aside and told him, "You're going to Ohio, man."

I didn't hear from him again for another year. He called to tell me his wife had left; she had taken their girls to Ohio and wasn't coming back. He talked of the situation: his grief, frustration, and powerlessness. I listened. After that, he called me occasionally, then regularly. He'd catch me up on his fractured marriage, and then we'd chat about other things: where we were going, where we'd been, the mundane details of our separate lives.

After my divorce I'd pretty much decided that my life was full enough with two kids and a career; that my job was to get my kids raised. Love could wait. Although I knew a lot of men and casually dated a few, I hadn't met anyone I was remotely interested in and certainly could not imagine bringing someone into my life with my kids. I didn't see myself as a woman needing a rescue, didn't have the skills or temperament to be coy, and wasn't very good at pretending I liked someone when I didn't. After my tumultuous childhood and difficult marriage, I was steeled. An iron maiden, my hard exterior protected my soft underbelly. That strength helped me succeed in navigating a complex work world. By the time I became reacquainted with Jeff, I was making a decent income directing a state agency and had recently bought my own house.

Although we had become friends over the telephone, I was nervous when Jeff wanted to come see me. He had a meeting in Baltimore, so he would be in the area for a couple of days. Although I liked him, I didn't know if there would be a spark, or what my reaction would be if there was one. I calmed myself by thinking that if there was no spark, that would be fine, too. I had some close male friends and valued their friendships immensely. The intimacy I felt with them, although not romantic, was both important and satisfying.

Jeff flew from Denver into Newark, New Jersey, rented a car, and showed up at my house in Delaware at one o'clock in the morning. I'd fallen asleep on the couch, and answered the door in my bathrobe, sans makeup, my hair in disarray. Jeff was standing on my porch with a bag in his hand and a big grin on his face.

We sat in the living room, both nervously reacquainting ourselves with each other in person. It was different from connecting as the disembodied voices we'd grown accustomed to. Jeff had lost weight since the last time I'd seen him—from the "divorce diet," he said—but looked good. I noticed his broad, muscular shoulders and the easy way he carried himself. He was dressed casually, but was neat and well groomed.

We sat for a long time, talking, and it was as if I saw Jeff for the first time. I noticed his green eyes, and his eyebrows that worked up and down as he observed things and mulled them over.

They moved when he was intent or amused, animating the calmness he otherwise exuded. That night they moved as he studied me. His gaze was strong and unbroken. His openness, directness, and artlessness rattled me, and sometimes I had to look away. Although our conversation was comfortable, there was an intensity I had not anticipated. I wasn't quite sure what to make of it, but whatever was going on, I was pretty sure I wasn't ready for it. The late night grew later, and we reluctantly took our leave from each other. I showed Jeff where he would sleep, and headed back to the couch.

The next morning, I got my children ready and off to school with their bags. Even though they remembered Jeff from our Colorado trip, they were still a little wiggy to see him in our house. Perhaps they felt something, too. They would be staying with their dad for the next few days, so I decided to go to Baltimore with Jeff for his meeting. I was familiar with the city and offered to show him the sights.

After Jeff's meeting, we hit a raw bar in the Cross Street Market, one of Baltimore's quaint old city markets. We ate oysters, drank beer, and talked some more. I was struck by how easy it was, how easy Jeff was as he slurped oysters from the shell, how easily he laughed. This guy from Montana, where the only oysters on the menu are the Rocky Mountain variety, had turned into a man who was comfortable in the world, at ease with himself. The warm feeling I'd begun to have for him the night before was getting warmer, perhaps assisted by the oysters.

After the oysters, we strolled through the market. Filled with stalls of flowers, fresh fruits and vegetables, meats, baked goods, and specialty items, the market had a unique Baltimore feel, reflecting its blue-collar, seaport history. After a while, I had to use the bathroom. I found it behind a booth, next to a smelly storage area, but the door was locked. Three old Baltimore characters who were shooting the breeze by the women's room door directed me to a nearby booth to get the key. Jeff stood off to the side, arms folded across his chest, his eyebrows working as I waited for the booth man to find the key. As I waited, I heard about all the things they had attached to the key to keep from losing it: a keychain, a ruler, a larger piece of wood, a hubcap. Finally he found it, attached to a large wooden buoy, making me wonder how the hell he could have misplaced it in the first place. I had to take the buoy with both hands, it was so heavy and cumbersome. I turned the key in the lock, held the door open with my rear end, set the buoy down on the ground, and dragged it into the bathroom behind me. Afterward, I repeated the aforementioned steps and lugged it back to the booth. It felt like there was a spotlight on me, a neon sign that registered to everyone in the whole place that I had just used the bathroom. Jeff and I had a good laugh.

We floated through the rest of the afternoon, and ended up in the waterfront neighborhood of Fell's Point to have dinner at Bertha's. It's an old restaurant, famous for mussels that come with a variety of delicious sauces for dipping. Bumper stickers from there say *Eat Bertha's Mussels,* and an entire wall of the bar is covered with bumper stickers that people have made from the original, all variations on the theme. They read *Eat Bertie's Bumples, Eat Bart's Shorts, Eat Lucille's Ball, Beat Bush's Ass, Eat Scooby's Doo,* and perhaps my favorite, *Free Clinton's Willy.* Amazing what people can do with some creativity and a pair of scissors.

We sat over mussels, talked of life, and fell in love. Jeff leaned forward, leaned into me as he talked about his children, his business, his goals and aspirations. He listened to my story, too. Occasionally he leaned back in the booth and laughed, but otherwise we were both fully engaged, leaning in. I was impressed by Jeff's devotion to his children, attitude about his business, and lack of bitterness. He was freshly and deeply wounded by his marriage falling apart and losing daily contact with his children, but of his wife, all he said was, "She did the best she could."

Over dinner and during the long drive back to my house, my mind wanted more of Jeff, and my heart was following right along. But with love, the body weighs in, too.

Although we both wanted to take things slowly, Jeff was scheduled to leave the next day. There was no time. Our lives were filled with complications of children, demanding careers, ex-spouses, and we were separated by miles and miles of geography. But as we fell into each other's arms, tentatively at first, the complications simply fell away. Something in me shifted, broke, and then broke open. My self-protective walls tumbled down, and the ice that had formed scar tissue in my heart began to melt: a glacial retreat. We were enveloped by a sort of liquid love that filled us up and spilled over into the room, the house, the world. This love did not feel of our own making. It came to us, fell on us, surrounded us, and entered deeply in. It was as if we were borne up by angels; our feet did not touch the ground.

Jeff changed his ticket, and we spent a week together floating in euphoria, Emmylou Harris's new release playing on repeat in the tape deck. As she sang about horses, we explored each other's territory; by the end of the week, we were hopelessly tethered, inextricably bound.

Then the panic set in. Nothing was right and everything was wrong about our situation. There were geographic impossibilities, and a load of baggage that seemed unbearably heavy. But after Jeff flew back to Denver, it became clear to me that if we listened to our fears or let reason prevail, we ran the risk of losing something precious and irreplaceable.

"What are we going to do?" Jeff asked me over the telephone. He was back home, and it was then that our cooler sides should have prevailed.

"I think we're going to get married," I said.

Jeff came to see me in January, in February, and in March. He introduced me to John Hiatt and Joe Jackson; I introduced him to Simply Red, Jane Siberry, and Crowded House, and we found we had a lot of music in common. In April, I flew out for a visit to Denver, and in May, Jeff moved himself and his business to Delaware. One of the first things we did was purchase a new gas grill to replace my ruined charcoal one. We went to one of those big hardware stores that used to be there before Home Depot drove them all out of business. As we were making our selection, I panicked.

"I'm not ready to buy a major appliance," I said. "We haven't even had a normal date yet, and we're already making a purchase of a jointly owned thing, and I don't think I can do it."

Jeff had to take me into another aisle to calm me down.

"It's a grill, Beth," he said. "It'll be okay. It's just a grill."

After we got in the car, we cracked up about my scene. It was just like the scene in that Jill Clayburgh movie *Starting Over*, when she and Burt Reynolds were shopping for a couch after they decided to try a life together. He had a panic attack and started hyperventilating, and when she asked the gathered onlookers if anyone had a Valium, *everyone* had a Valium.

∾

That night in Chautauqua, the concert exceeded our expectations. Emmylou Harris' voice blended with and rose above the music of the guitars and mandolins. She played some of her new songs, but did the old ones, too. The amphitheater is open, with a high wooden roof supported by tall pillars. A large stage at one end is surrounded by tiered rows of long, old church pews, painted white, reminiscent of the Ryman Theater in Nashville. One of the world's largest pipe organs is behind the stage. Used during church services, it provides a striking backdrop for other performances. The acoustics are perfect, and the sound stays true even as it continues to fill the air outside the facility itself. I once heard Jane Goodall do her chimpanzee call here, and it sent a chill up my spine. Emmylou Harris's heartbreaking voice did the same.

After the concert, Jeff and I walked down the brick path toward the lake. We wiped the dew off the seats and settled into the boat for the ride home.

Stars extended to the horizon and formed an infinite canopy above us.

"Drive slow," I said, tilting my head back to look up. "I want to watch the sky."

"It looks just like the skies used to look in Montana," Jeff said. "Millions of stars."

We slowly made our way across the lake, drinking in the silence under the Chautauqua sky that *is* the Montana sky, quietly thinking our own thoughts. It was as if our shared and separate histories, our present and our future came together in a singular moment. At the dock, Jeff helped me out of the boat and kept my hand. We crossed the wide lawn together and went inside.

In a Town This Size

There isn't much to be seen in a little town, but what you hear makes up for it.

—Kin Hubbard

We didn't want to miss anything happening at the lake if we could help it, so we drove up to spend our first Fourth of July weekend as owners. Jeff wanted to fish, but I wanted to get to know everybody. By the same token, people were curious about us. Some kept their distance, cautiously assessing us to see if we were friendly, or perhaps didn't belong. Others were immediately warm, occasionally overly warm, raising our own suspicions. But whether they warmed to us quickly or grew on us over time, the friendly people were a big part of what had attracted us to the lake.

As we had learned, part of the everyday rhythm of life in Maple Springs included a chat with Spike to catch up on the news. He drove to the lakefront in his old truck early every morning to gossip, and to go over his boats in case someone came by to rent. When he wasn't jawboning, he spent his time picking up sticks, raking lake weeds, burying dead fish, mowing, or pushing things around with his big green tractor. He was perpetual motion, running around on bowed legs, smoking his corncob pipe. It was as if he opened the lake in the morning and put it safely to bed each night.

As soon as we pulled in, Spike came running to fill us in on what we'd missed while we'd been gone. "George Whitbeck caught some nice walleye last week," he said after a warm hello. "And a muskie. A 48-incher. Jeff, have I ever showed you my muskie lures? I have a bunch of them in the shuffleboard."

After Spike sold the old Whiteside hotel, he retained a small piece of land just off the lake. He used it to store his boats, tractor, materials and supplies for his boat rental and worm business. Depending on the season, Spike's lot could get pretty littered with chairs, equipment, spare parts, and boats in various stages of disintegration. The neighborhood bitched about him "squatting" on the lakefront, and about his property. They complained it was an eyesore, but it was just part of the landscape to us. It was really just a vacant lot, with a long, low shed that was caving in on itself. When the hotel was operational, the grassy lot was a tennis court, and the shed housed the shuffleboard court. The Kelderhouses and the old-timers who remembered the hotel still referred to the shed as the "shuffleboard."

We extricated ourselves from Spike and began unloading the car. The girls ran upstairs to unpack their suitcases and sort their things into drawers while Jeff and I managed the rest. We hauled in our suitcases, extra pillows, groceries, and a new tube for pulling the girls on the water. Butch caught us in the parking lot.

"Marge and I talked it over," he said, "and even though it's a break with tradition, we thought it would be a good idea to have a party on the lakefront on the Fourth. We always get together on Labor Day, but usually people celebrate the Fourth with their own guests and families. There are people you should meet, and lots of the neighbors want to meet you and the O'Connors. They want to inspect the new owners."

"That sounds like fun," I said. "What can we bring?"

"You and Margie can coordinate," Butch said. "Of course, you and your girls will sit at our table."

"I don't know how much time we can count on with the girls," Jeff said. "They're getting to be teenagers, and don't want to spend that much time with us anymore. They won't miss out on the food, but don't be surprised if we don't see much of them."

"There have been some boys skateboarding in the parking lot all week," Butch said. "I thought about running them off, but they seemed nice and polite. I checked them out. They're about the same age as your girls."

"Ugh," Jeff said, rolling his eyes. Although he was beginning to get used to it, he didn't like the idea of boys around our girls.

The day of the party was beautiful and sunny. The sky was a real sky blue, with fat white clouds floating high. A Simpson's sky, I call it, since it looks like the sky in the opening credits of the cartoon show. We helped Butch and Marge set up a big plastic table, and watched as several neighbors hauled tables and chairs to the lakefront. News of the party spread by word of mouth, and by two o'clock people started gathering.

From the start, Butch and Marge helped us get established in the community. They knew the history of the townhouses well and had spent years on Chautauqua Lake as owners and as visitors. Butch had retired as an engineer for a steel company, and he was always tinkering with something. He taught Jeff the inner workings of the building: how the heating systems worked, the mysteries of the pump room, the workings of the wells, left over from the hotel. They invited us for happy hours on their pontoon boat, which we dubbed "Marge's Barge," and introduced us to many of their friends and neighbors. They were warm and open, always genuinely interested in our accomplishments and our difficulties. Over time, we grew to love them as friends even though they were quite a bit older than we.

Butch introduced us to George and Sandra Whitbeck, who had their table outfitted with a beautiful cloth, a flower-filled vase, crystal, and china. George, tall and loose-limbed, was a retired chef, and brought out stuffed cherry tomatoes as an appetizer, the platter decorated with fern leaves from his garden. Although he sometimes wore what looked to be a scowl on his face, throughout the afternoon we could hear George's booming laughter erupt. His wife, Sandra, was harder to read. She was quiet, but her eyes sparkled as if she'd just swallowed a joke.

Spike showed up with his wife, also named Sandy, whom he married after Norma died. We'd seen her sitting in Spike's truck some evenings, but she rarely ventured out. Younger than Spike, she was mousy and quiet, with a limp, fishy handshake. Spike wore pressed clothes for the occasion and smelled of men's cologne.

With the crowd gathering, it looked as if we needed more side tables, so I ran to the townhouse to retrieve an old metal TV tray I'd picked up earlier that summer at the big antique store in Salamanca, on the Seneca Indian reservation. I hollered to the girls that dinner would be ready soon and brought the table outside. I set it up by our chairs, and soon Spike and Butch came over to admire it. The top of the tray showed a Florida scene of blue skies, water, and a woman in a two-piece bathing suit, circa early sixties, leaning against a mangrove tree. Lettering across the top identified the table as a souvenir from Silver Springs.

"Oh, I like that table! Have you ever been to Silver Springs?" Butch asked, turning to Spike.

"Oh, yes, oh, yes," said Spike. "I was stationed near there when I was in the Air Corps, before I went to Greenland. That's where they have those glass-bottom boats. Did you ever go on one? Ever see them Weeki Wachee mermaids?"

"I sure did," said Butch. "When I was a young man. It's not far from our place in New Smyrna Beach. It's not the same as it was, though."

As Butch and Spike continued reminiscing, it slowly dawned on me that they weren't admiring my table. They were admiring the girl in the yellow bathing suit and remembering themselves as young men. Jeff, his eyebrows working up and down with amusement, figured it out before I did. He had heard his own dad and his buddies talk about Weeki Wachee girls at the American Legion and later at the Good Time Club, a private club that Jeff's parents and their cronies started and ran in upstate New York after they couldn't drink at the fire hall anymore. And now here we were, with Butch and Spike, a couple of old ducks with their tongues practically hanging out over a faded picture of a young woman in a modest yellow bathing suit. Even though the Weeki Wachees may have lost their allure in our modern culture, some things never change.

I scanned the lakefront, taking in all the people and trying to remember names. There were no Weeki Wachee girls in sight. Spike leaned into his wife, Sandy, and asked her if she wanted something else to drink. In spite of the noisy appreciation of the Weeki

Wachees, and perhaps even the comparisons, like the rest of the men, he seemed grateful for the warm comfort of his imperfect wife.

Marge jolted me out of my reverie when she called us over to eat. The table was lovely. She had placed some zinnias from the front garden into a blue pitcher, and set out colorful plates. Her husband, Butch, tended the front gardens, where he planted zinnias, peonies, daisies, and lilies. She looked much younger than her years. Very trim, she moved with the grace of a young woman although she was over seventy. Marge wore a tiny bracelet around her ankle, and polished toenails peeked out of her sandals.

I went around back to get the girls. Lisa and Maggie were standing in the parking lot talking with the boys who had returned with their skateboards, while Kayla, too young for them, sat on the porch with a miserable look on her face. "The girls have to eat now," I said to the boys. "But you can come back later if you want. They should be finished in about an hour."

We sat down next to Butch, and Jeff sat down between Butch and Marge. An older man, tall and thin, wearing large sunglasses, asked if he could take the remaining seat. He was clean-shaven, but patches of whiskers stuck out of the spots he'd missed. The skin on his face was loose, and a network of broken capillaries covered his nose and cheeks.

"Oh, yes, yes, Tom, please join us," Butch said, and introduced us to Tom Cummiskey. I knew he had one of the docks on the lakefront, and although I'd seen him toddling around on the lawn with his little schnauzer, we'd not yet met.

"Tom lives in the big house, on the circle," Butch said.

"I've admired your house," I told him. It was a tall, two-story Victorian, with a large porch across the front. The roof of the porch was sagging and plants grew out of the upper gutters, but the place was still attractive.

"I've admired your boat," Tom said. "I had an old boat like that, before I bought my new one. I named it *The Drain* because I was always pouring money into it. Yes, I think I'll have a little wine," he said when Butch offered. Butch passed the bottle.

"My house is actually a cottage," Tom said. "No foundation. You'll have to stop over and see it."

I walked over to the food table with Tom and we loaded our plates with corn and salads.

"I made these beans," Tom said.

I helped myself and offered him some chicken that Jeff had grilled earlier. My appetizer was still sitting there, looking sorrier the longer the party went on. For Christmas, Jeff had given me the double set of Julia Child's *The Art of French Cooking*, autographed, and I was so overcome, I didn't just get misty, I boohooed. But the only cookbook I had at the lake was one I picked up at a flea market, an old one called *Great Recipes from the World's Great Cooks*. I had decided to try something exotic: strawberries filled with caviar, sprinkled with vodka and a little lime juice. As the afternoon wore on, the strawberries grew dull while the caviar got shinier. Those little eggs were either growing salmonella or getting closer to hatching. Tom looked at them with interest.

"I made these," I said. "I'm afraid they might be a mistake."

"Let's take them to the table," he said. "I want to try them."

We settled back in at the table. Tom took a strawberry and passed the dish over to Marge. She popped one into her mouth, made a face, and promptly spit it out onto her plate.

"They might be better if they were still chilled," I said lamely.

"I like them," Tom said. "But I love caviar."

"I won't be making them again," I said. "And it looks like I'll have to work hard to keep up with George Whitbeck. His appetizer was great."

"I'm glad you won't make them again," Marge said, laughing. "I might barf."

Hoping to change the subject, I asked Tom what he did.

"I'm a retired physician," he said. "Radiologist, to be exact, although I practiced internal medicine before that. I'm still active on the board of the Medical Society, but during the summer I try to spend as much time down here as I can."

Tom spoke slowly in a deep voice, enunciating his words perfectly. Over the course of the meal, and with a little more wine, he loosened up a bit and told a couple of pretty good jokes. His formal demeanor was often punctuated by his easy laughter.

"Hey, Doc." Jesse Kelderhouse, one of Spike's sons, stopped by our table and waved away my offer of food. His long T-shirt covered his big belly and most of his shorts. "I ate already," he said. "Now I'm just working on a beer. A few beers."

Tom stood up and excused himself. "Need to stretch my legs," he said. "I'll return shortly."

The girls asked to be excused.

"Why don't you go over and say hello to the O'Connors before you go back in the house?" Jeff said. "They have some room at their table. You don't have to stay long. Those boys don't seem to be going anywhere, at least not until I run them off."

"Tom seems like an interesting man," I said to Jesse as the girls got up.

"Yeah, Doc's okay." He took a swig of beer. "Did you hear about the time that he and his sister took *The Drain* out? When they got back they were so drunk, they got out of the boat and fell off the dock into the water. One on each side. That sister's dead now, but he's got another one. She's a real doozie, too."

It was a stretch to imagine this dignified doctor drunk and floundering in the lake. As I tried to picture it in my mind, the whole scene on the lakefront struck me. Young people and old gathered together; children and grandchildren playing on the lawn; pedestrians strolling down the road were waved over to join the party; even a couple of dogs joined in the fun. The trappings of normal life that denote status, class, and power seemed to have slipped into a vague background. Status in the community seemed to have as much to do with relationship to the lake, or whether or not a person could figure out docks, lifts, and motors, as it did with title or resources. Despite the closeness of the group, built on shared history, I felt welcomed, and I could see Jeff felt the same. Neither he nor I had experienced anything like it since we were children: he with his parents and their friends in upstate New York, me at my grandparents' house in Omaha. Even at that first party I had a sense of respect for the old guard: Butch, Spike, Doc Cummiskey, and others. They kept things stable and maintained the traditions that held the community together. They implicitly set the standards for acceptable behavior: how one treated the lake and the neighbors was the important thing. The size of the car, the boat, or the cottage was immaterial.

Jeff had been staring at the lake. Suddenly he pointed at something. "What's that?" he asked.

Butch followed his gesture and laughed. "That's the Viking sailboat."

The boat was large, a replica Viking ship, overly embellished, with a garish dragon figurehead on its prow and large, wind-filled sails.

"The Viking Club is right next to Midway," Butch continued. "Every few years they get the boat from Lake Erie, I think, for Scandinavian Days. Only members can ride on it."

"Emil and Betty belong to the Viking Club," said Marge. "But I don't think they take the cruise anymore. Everyone dresses up in costumes and drinks beer—it's like a floating beer party. They eat Körv and pickled herring. Disgusting. Have you met Emil and Betty yet? They live in the little cottage behind us, the one that looks like a gingerbread house. Come on, I'll introduce you."

She led us over to a big table and introduced us to Emil and Betty Arvidson. Emil stood up, shook Jeff's hand, and planted a big kiss full on my mouth.

"Whoa," I said as I disengaged myself. "Pleased to meet you."

Emil introduced us to his twin brother, Eric. They were identical, slightly built, with frayed, reddish hair running to gray. They both wore the same style of glasses. Eric was a little heavier, softer, and his skin sagged a bit more. Otherwise they were impossible to tell apart.

"Betty always brings Swedish meatballs to these parties," Marge said on the way back to our table. "And Eric's wife is German. She always brings German chocolate cake."

We sat listening to the swirling voices and absorbing more neighborhood history: "Jesse Kelderhouse can certainly drink some beer . . . For a while, a man rented one of the townhouses and kept his mistress in it . . . I heard that somebody might buy the old general store; that place has been closed for years . . . You know them, Jeff, you bought your townhouse from them . . . Dick Reitler was a full colonel in the Air Force, a decorated war veteran . . . Rosemary was a nun before she married Dick . . . he played football with the Steelers . . . The Walshes are still trying to sell Midway Park . . . There's a cottage for sale on the Rivulet, but they're asking way too much money for it . . ." And on and on and on.

Later that afternoon Jeff and I retreated to debrief and rest up in preparation for the evening activities. We had two couches set up at right angles in our living room; they formed a nice seating arrangement for visiting and were perfect for tandem napping. Almost as soon as Jeff closed his eyes, his breathing became slow and regular, lulling me toward sleep.

"I couldn't help picturing Betty in a Viking getup on that boat," I said to Jeff. "With blond braids and one of those hats with horns on it."

Jeff snorted. "That boat looked great out on the water. You know, I think I like these people."

"I know what you mean. It's starting to feel like we belong," I said, and then we drifted off to sleep.

As it began to grow dark, neighbors assembled again on the lakefront. Someone started a fire in the fire pit. We went outside with the girls. On the Fourth of July, Midway has a fireworks display that is visible from the townhouses, but we decided to take in the show from the lake, on the boat.

Butch and Spike were arranging flares every few feet along the shoreline.

"At ten o'clock," Butch said, "the whole lake will light up. Everyone lights flares along the shoreline, and then the fireworks start."

Flares are for sale for the Fourth of July at little stores and gas stations all over the lake. The do-gooders bitch about the flares, since they release a little bit of phosphorous that ends up in the lake, but the sale of the flares benefits the fire department. Besides, it's a long tradition, and people are reluctant to buck tradition, especially a nostalgic one, in this old-fashioned place.

We walked down the dock, and the girls and I got in the boat. We all had on sweatshirts; it had grown chilly since the sun went down. Jeff lowered the boat into the water and climbed in. He slowly backed out of the lift, and we headed toward Midway. Other people got in their boats, too, but some, including Butch and Spike, stayed on the shore to light the flares.

The water was calm as we rounded the bend toward the open water in front of Midway. The sky was clear, with a million twinkling stars layered on top of each other. Away from city lights, the night sky was astonishing. I pointed out different planets and constellations to the girls: Venus, the Dippers, the Pleiades, and Orion. We could see the thick sweep of stars that form the Milky Way.

We picked a spot and lowered the anchor to wait. It seemed that everyone had the same idea. There were pontoons, speedboats, cabin cruisers, ski boats, fishing boats, and a couple of big boats that looked out of place, like they belonged on the ocean. Some people were tied up with friends, rubber bumpers preventing their boats from making direct contact. The sound on the water is different than it is on land. Even though talking, laughter, and music floated all around us, it seemed very quiet, water lapping gently against the boat.

Jeff and I each opened a beer. The girls had ginger ales and dug into a bag of chips they'd brought. I leaned my head back and breathed in the stars.

"Look," Kayla said. She was pointing across the lake, where a cluster of flares blazed. In a minute, the whole lake was ringed with pink light. People in the boats started whooping and blowing their horns.

The fireworks went off shortly after. It was a decent fireworks show, professionally done, and all the more thrilling because of the accompanying ooohs, aaahs, and applause. After the finale, someone lit a huge bonfire on shore that looked like it would be dangerous if it were to topple. The light from the bonfire illuminated people's faces in an odd, flickering way as we glided toward home.

"That was great," Jeff said later, as we were settling in for the night.

"The whole thing's great," I said. "The girls had a good time. It doesn't seem to take much of an excuse to have a picnic or a party around here. These people are pretty gossipy, though. It makes you wonder what they're saying about us."

"I think the ones we like are just talking about our boat," Jeff said.

"Seriously, Jeff," I said, "there's something about this place that is really drawing me in. The old-timey rituals here remind me of my grandparents. They always had picnics on the summer holidays. We picnicked on Memorial Day, and there was always a picnic on the Fourth of July. We'd light fireworks. Their friends would come, and all my aunts, uncles, and cousins."

"I like it, too," he said. "The flares and fires are kind of corny, but nice. It's so hard to have family traditions with the kids coming and going like they do."

"Maybe some of this easy structure will rub off on them," I said. "We can build our own traditions with them up here, without having to accommodate everybody else." I turned out my light and rolled over to sleep.

Lake Time

We have so much time and so little to do. Strike that, reverse it.

—Willy Wonka (Roald Dahl)

Time passes in funny ways at the lake. It is both compressed and expanded. It unfolds in odd and mysterious ways. Because it is primarily a summer community, we cram our visits into a lovely few weeks. The years between the summers pass by with a whisper. Days go by just as strangely. Sometimes they stretch out long before us; other times it is suddenly dusk and we've had no time to eat. A trip to the post office can take all morning; checking on the boat can take all afternoon. A stroll through the neighborhood can result in hours visiting with people on their porches; an afternoon with a book can last forever. Yet the summers are over in the blink of an eye.

Plans often change because of the way time passes here. Our plans to leave might be delayed for hours by a quick chat with someone that turns into a neighborhood confab. Days designated for chores are interrupted by a neighbor's request for help with something, or by weather so glorious we're compelled to jump in the boat. Something funny or odd happens on the lakefront; suddenly the day is gone and the grocery shopping hasn't been done. Sometimes the day starts out with an interruption, the interruption becomes the day, and the days become the life at the lake.

The Labor Day party on the lakefront is an annual tradition. The whole neighborhood gathers on the wide lawn in front of the townhouses to celebrate and mourn the end of the short summer. People roll their grills around front and carry their tables, picnic gear, and food to the party in wheelbarrows. Some people bring linens, vases filled with flowers, crystal wine glasses, and china, while others settle for paper plates and beer in ice-filled buckets.

Labor Day marks the end of summer here, and not just because the children go back to school and the summer people return to their regular lives. It is as if God uses a stopwatch: whether the summer is cool or hot as blazes, whether we wear shorts or sweatshirts to the picnic, the day after is autumn. Even if the days stay warm, the nights are cool, and the leaves start turning and dropping from the trees. Some years, the day after Labor Day is the day one must bring out the winter clothes, don sweaters, socks, and hats. We pull them off again during Indian summer days throughout the fall, but they must remain in easy reach through May and sometimes into June.

One year, the party had a theme: *A Garden Party—Think Monet* was on the flier that our neighbor, Linda O'Connor, handed out or stuffed inside screen doors. Several of the women showed up in gauzy dresses, and George Whitbeck wore a white seersucker suit and sported a boater hat and a big cigar. As usual, George brought a delicious dish to share: a dip made with soft cheeses and fresh herbs. Sandra Whitbeck and her sister Joan, whom everyone calls

Queenie, were all decked out, ready to eat, gossip, and laugh. I placed my own contribution, Texas Caviar with Fritos Scoops, on the appetizer table. It's a simple recipe, doesn't wilt in the heat, and always gets gobbled up.

I waved at Emil and Betty Arvidson, who were sitting with their relatives at one of the tables that held their usual Swedish meatballs and German chocolate cake. We could see their little cottage from our back porch. It is tiny, with cedar shake siding, and it looks like a gingerbread house with a ballooned roof and an eyebrow dormer over the front porch. In his early seventies, Emil is thin and wiry. Betty is older, over eighty, and heavier.

"I wish I'd brought a dress and hat," said my mom, who was visiting for the long weekend. "Everybody looks great."

"I can get you a hat," said Shirley Nook, who leads the sing-along every year. Shirley lives next door to Emil and Betty, and was wearing a festive hat herself. She returned after a few minutes carrying a wide-brimmed straw hat, with little crocheted pom-poms hanging off the rim.

"Now I'm set," my mom said, laughing as she donned the hat.

Jeff and I sat down with George Whitbeck to catch up on the news.

"Emil and Betty invited us for breakfast at the Viking Club last weekend," Jeff said. "But we had to pay. I couldn't believe it."

"They stiffed us, but it was fun," I chimed in. "Emil kept his hands in his pockets when it came time to cough up the money for breakfast. Even though they invited us to *their* club. The Vikings were eating pancakes and cracking beers at nine o'clock in the morning."

George laughed and took a long pull on his cigar. "The Scandinavians are thrifty. But the Vikings' isn't one of those fancy clubs where they frown on people paying for things. Sandra and I are members. We pay an annual fee, but otherwise, everything is cash. No accounts. We'll take you sometime, but it will be Dutch treat."

"I guess we misunderstood, then," I said. "It was only five bucks, but it was still a little awkward."

"Emil and Betty invited us over for drinks one night," he continued. "And do you know what they served us? Crème de Menthe! That's all they had, ferchri'sakes, Crème de Menthe. Scandinavians are thrifty—they're Lutherans!" George's laugh boomed out.

After the desserts, Shirley Nook started herding us next door to the sweeping, pillared front porch of the Whiting's Victorian house, passing out copies of sheet music and lyrics for the sing-along.

"We'll start with 'A Bicycle Built for Two,'" Shirley said after we got settled. Then she called out a long note for pitch and raised her hands, conductorlike. She led the song in a maniacally jovial and assertive way, raising her arms up and down with a wild look in her eyes until we got to the end, when she dropped them to a full stop.

"'In the Good Old Summertime'!" she announced enthusiastically, and we all joined in, glancing at the lyrics while Shirley flailed her arms to keep time.

Under my breath, I whispered alternative words to Jeff while Shirley led us through "My Bonnie Lies Over the Ocean": ". . . My Bonnie has tuberculosis . . . My Bonnie has only one lung . . . My Bonnie spits blood in a bucket . . . and dries it and chews it for gum."

Jeff struggled to stifle his laughter and finally got it under control when the cameras came out for the group picture. People handed their cameras to Linda O'Connor's dad, who took pictures while we posed. The steps, flanked by huge rhododendrons, held all of us for the singing, and the terracing effect of the stairs ensured that even the short people got in the photograph.

I have a lot of those pictures now, taped up inside my Hoosier cabinet after spending their allotted time on the refrigerator. Doc Cummiskey in his big sunglasses; Butch and Marge, sometimes with their kids and grandkids; the Whitbecks with and without their clan; the Nooks; the O'Connors, their small kids now big kids; the Ferrises; various Kelderhouses; Ryan Sullivan; Emil and Betty; the Solomons. People who come, and people who go; all the major and minor characters who are part of our life at the lake. We have pictures from the Labor Day party with the Woodstock theme: Mike O'Connor in a spangled headband; Sandra Whitbeck in tie-dye and love beads, a Post-it Note rolled like a joint, held together with a hair clip; George Whitbeck in a wig, looking like a forlorn, washed-up rock star; Jeff wearing a leather vest over a *Jesus Christ Superstar* T-shirt; me with dangling earrings, bangles on my wrists and a rhinestone brooch that reads *Dick Nixon*. All of us from the townhouses. Old friends and new friends, all part of this grand and goofy tradition.

$\sim$

The morning after the Labor Day party, my mom and I were relaxing in the townhouse when the phone rang. It was Emil Arvidson.

"Betty and I left a blue plate and a cheese knife out front when we left the party yesterday," he said. "I was wondering if you could go check and see if they're still there."

"Sure," I said. "I'll run out right now. What do they look like?"

"The cheese knife has a blue handle, and the plate is blue, triangle-shaped."

"Okay," I said. "Let me check, and I'll call you right back."

I told my mother what was going on and went outside. The lakefront was cool and cloudy, still socked in with fog as it sometimes is on fall mornings. The far shore had vanished, and it was eerie and still. Sounds carried in unexpected ways, muffled and amplified at the same time. Fishing conversations floated by from invisible boats, and the cries of loons and gulls resonated elliptically so I couldn't tell if they were coming from close in or from miles away.

There were still a couple of tables set up from the day before, and beer bottles littered the ground where the chairs circled the fire pit by the water. I picked up some of the bottles and straightened chairs as I moved my way across the grounds, snippets of conversations and events from the day before swirling through my mind. I waved at the O'Connor girls, who were playing a game on the floor behind their screen door.

I located a flowered plastic tray on one of the picnic tables and turned it over to see if there was a name on it, but there wasn't. I picked it up to bring it into the house, and noticed a cheese knife on the ground next to the table. It had a blue handle, so I figured it was Emil's, but I didn't see a blue plate.

When I got inside, I rang Emil back.

"I got the knife, Emil, but I couldn't find the plate," I said. "My mom and I are getting ready to eat, so I'll run it up to you later on."

I scrambled some eggs to go with our bagels, and my mom and I sat down to eat. We were planning to do a little shopping at Skillman's in Bemus Point that afternoon and then stop by Haff Acres for some fruits, vegetables, and a pie for dessert. I said I hoped the weather cleared, that it looked like the fog was beginning to burn off.

"If there's enough blue in the sky to stitch a man's shirt, it will clear," said my mom.

I heard Emil knocking on the sliding door and went out, still chewing the last of my breakfast. "Hey, Emil," I said. "I told you I'd run that stuff up."

My mom came out to greet Emil and settled into a porch chair with her coffee.

I handed him the cheese knife and the plastic tray and he looked them over. "Yup, this is our knife." After long minutes studying the tray, turning it over and over, taking in all the angles, he said, "This isn't our tray. I don't know who it belongs to."

Emil stood there for a few more minutes. I offered him a cup of coffee and a seat, which he waved away. "I wonder what happened to that plate," he said.

"I'll keep my eye out for it," I assured him.

"You're sure you didn't see it?" he asked, scanning the lakefront himself. "I wonder where it got off to."

"I think I looked everywhere," I said. "Maybe someone took it by mistake, or took it home to wash and will bring it back."

I tried not to look at my mom but could see her eyebrows go up as the minutes continued to tick by, with Emil standing there, holding his cheese knife but not his blue plate, looking defeated.

After a while, I asked, "Is the plate solid blue?" In my mind I was picturing Wedgewood, Delft, a cobalt transfer pattern, or some other heirloom-quality china.

"Yes, solid blue," he said. "It's a blue plastic plate, triangle-shaped. Maybe you could ask around, see if anybody else found it."

Out of the corner of my eye, I could see my mom's eyes widen as it dawned on both of us that all this time and effort was going into finding a plastic plate. Blue plastic.

While Emil continued to stand on the porch, Betty came into view, slowly making her way across the lawn, pushing, and then leaning on her walker. Her legs were bare and swollen under billowing blue shorts; the skin over her ankles was irritated, stretched tight. Loose moccasins covered her feet. She inched along, each step excruciatingly slow, taking tiny steps, tiny, shuffling steps. Her feet seemed stuck and didn't lift off the ground. The tiny tiny steps eventually added up to a little forward motion. Shuffle, shuffle, humph and glide. The rest of Betty was stiff and still; all of her energy and concentration was going into those tiny steps. She looked up and her eyes locked onto us in a form of greeting, although her face remained expressionless and stony.

Betty suffers from a chronic and progressive neurological disorder characterized by a variety of symptoms: a flat, masklike expression, slow gait and unsteadiness, and getting stuck or "freezing" while walking. The worst thing about it, perhaps, is the difficulty she has communicating. Even though she has a quick wit and loves to laugh, it takes time for the words to form, or for her to register a response at all. It was very sad and difficult to watch Betty's slow decline. That day, her trip to my porch took a really, really long time.

When she finally arrived, Emil repeated the whole story, replete with details, about my finding the cheese knife but not the blue plate. Betty listened intently, looking disappointed. She had made a long journey from her house to mine, by herself, to get the blue plate, but it wasn't here. Even though they had the cheese knife, it just wasn't enough.

I could see my mom sit up straighter in her chair so she didn't miss anything, and knew by the look on her face that she was ready to burst over how ridiculous this whole blue-plate situation was becoming. It was taking hours. It was right out of the *Andy Griffith Show*, where Floyd the Barber's misplaced comb takes up the entire episode, things are repeated over and over, *but nothing happens.* My mom swallowed her laugh but kept a bemused and very alert expression on her face while she sipped her coffee, and I could see her getting fidgety because the lost blue plate was starting to cut into our shopping time.

After a few more minutes, filled with long silences and more details about the futile efforts to find the plate, Emil turned to help Betty so they could leave. Just then I remembered the hat my mom had borrowed from Shirley Nook, their neighbor, for the party, and ran into the house to get it.

"Can you take this hat back to Shirley?" I asked.

Up to then, Betty had been silent, but suddenly she blurted out, "That's not Shirley's hat."

"Yes, it is," I told her. "Shirley loaned it to my mom for the party."

"Shirley had on a hat with flowers," said Betty, eyeing the pom-poms. "This is not Shirley's hat."

Betty was deadpan because of her condition. I saw my mom shift, turn, and fidget in her chair, trying to keep herself under control. At this point, we were both anticipating a few more hours of conversation about the silly hat.

"This isn't the hat that Shirley wore to the party," I explained. "It's a different hat, one that Shirley loaned to Mom. It's still Shirley's hat. It's Shirley's *other* hat."

My mom started babbling about how nice Shirley was to go get her the hat, and how much she appreciated being able to wear the hat because of the theme of the party and because she looks good in hats but never gets to wear them. I was ready to shoot her a look so she would *shut up* because everybody was already pretty confused, when Emil said he would take the hat back to Shirley.

"You call me if you find that plate," he said. "I think I'll go up to the post office and put a note on the bulletin board, in case someone else finds it."

My mom and I watched as they made their slow way home, Emil carrying the cheese knife and Shirley's hat. We bagged the shopping trip because of time, but we did make it to Haff Acres for some pie. Later on, we walked to the post office to see if the note about the blue plate was there, but the only note on the board was about Colleen O'Connor's missing left shoe.

Betty is still with us, but she is struggling terribly. Emil is struggling, too. He takes loving care of her, and brings her down in the car to sit by the lake. Betty loves the lake. Her blue eyes still sparkle with humor, but she is having more difficulty speaking, and it makes Emil lonely. Maybe if we had found that blue plate, Betty wouldn't be so sick. Sometimes when the big things are beyond our control, managing the little things helps. That blue plate never did turn up.

Life at the lake goes on; the great wheel keeps turning. We share it with each other here in Maple Springs, no matter what we lose, or what we find.

Irises in the Rivulet, Maple Springs. *Author photo.*

Tundra Swan in the Rivulet, Maple Springs. *Author photo.*

The Chautauqua Belle, an authentic Mississippi River-style sternwheel steamboat, is reminiscent of the steamers that transported passengers to their destinations around the lake before the automobile. It is one of only five operating steamboats of its type in North America. Built in 1975 in Mayville, the ship was launched in 1976 to mark the celebration of America's Bicentennial. *Photo by Randall Burt, courtesy of Captain Mat Stage.*

Christopher Whitbeck (holding muskie), Hunter Whitbeck. *Courtesy George and Sandra Whitbeck.*

Miller Bell Tower, Chautauqua Institution, Winter, 2008. *Courtesy Tony Giammarise.*

Viking Ship on Chautauqua Lake. *Author photo.*

Labor Day Party. *Author photo.*

Front row, standing, left to right: Betty Arvidson, Kathryn O'Connor with Cubby, Mrs. Eric Arvidson, Eric Arvidson

Front row, seated: Kyle Jacoby, Shirley Nook, Jennifer Whitbeck Schnell

Second row seated: Marilyn Martin, David Schnell holding Zachary, Sandra Whitbeck holding Teresa, Jean Jacoby, Colleen O'Connor

Third row: Emil Arvidson, standing, George Whitbeck, Tricia Jacoby

Group in the back: Doug Martin, Emily Baumgartner, Keith Martin, Bob Waddell, Joan "Queenie" Leskiw, Ryan Sullivan, Marge Waddell, Joan Sullivan, Bill Nook, Beth Peyton, Jeff Hunter, Pete Jacoby, Linda O'Connor's mom, Mike O'Connor, Linda O'Connor

Spike Kelderhouse holding Jeff Kelderhouse, 1955. *Courtesy Jeff Kelderhouse.*

Spike Kelderhouse. *Photo by Jane Currie, courtesy Jevin Kelderhouse.*

Old Maple Springs Fire Hall and Truck. Author's House in the Background. *Courtesy Maple Springs Fire Department.*

Ice Melting on Chautauqua Lake, Spring 2011. *Author photo.*

Henry on the Dock. Maple Springs.

Jesse Kelderhouse (standing) and Jevin Kelderhouse (seated) ice fishing on Chautauqua Lake. *Author photo.*

Bodies

Here lies one whose name was writ on water.

—John Keats

Although I loved Jeff, I didn't love the boat. Something was always breaking, and the ride was rough unless we went slowly. Since the boat was so important to him, I tried to endure, but I wasn't always enthusiastic about taking it out, especially on rough days. It wasn't until I learned to drive the boat that I began to love it, too.

"It's just like driving a car," Jeff said as he adjusted various knobs and checked fluid levels. He pulled a knob on the dashboard out and pushed it back in again. "We've got almost half a tank of gas. Don't leave this knob out while you're driving, or after you shut the boat off," he continued. "It drains the battery."

I was sitting in the driver's seat, but Jeff was moving all around me while the lift lowered us into the water.

"Before you start it, you pump this bulb," Jeff said, holding a black thing attached to the motor in the back. "Just pump it until it's hard. Okay, the propeller's in the water, so you can start it. Keep it in neutral."

I turned the key, but the engine didn't catch.

"Give it a little gas," he said.

"How do I do that?"

"Just a sec," he said as he got out of the boat to turn off the lift. He climbed back in and hovered over me.

"This is the throttle," he said. "Push it to give it gas, and to go forward. Pull it backward to make the boat go into reverse. This little flapperdoodle puts it in neutral. This switch here raises and lowers the motor."

"Where's the brake?" I asked.

"Boats don't have brakes," he laughed. "You just ease up on the throttle to slow it down, and put it in reverse if you want to do a complete stop."

"I don't see how it can be just like driving a car if it doesn't have any fucking brakes," I said. I'd been in the boat with him a lot, hadn't noticed him going through all this rigmarole, and was getting nervous and cranky.

The engine caught, and I put the boat in reverse.

"You've got to give it a little more gas to get it off the lift," Jeff said. "Slow down! Slow down!" he said after I did, and we were in the water. "Go forward, go forward!" he screamed. "You're going to hit the dock!"

I managed to pull the boat away from the dock and into more open water. By this time I was shaking. Jeff droned on about the rules of the water, who has the right-of-way and under what conditions, the colors of the lights and what they mean, blah, blah, blah. Jeff really did want me to drive the boat, but in his enthusiasm he couldn't help acting like Mister Know-It-All, and I was getting annoyed.

"Watch out for that boat," Jeff said, and jumped up to grab the steering wheel. In the process, he elbowed me in the head and stepped on my foot.

"I saw it," I said. "I wasn't even near it. You drive now. I'm not having any fun."

I was determined to drive the boat, even though it scared me witless. No brakes, deep water, and if I fell out of it, I wasn't sure if I could get back in. But I planned to be at the lake without Jeff, by myself, with kids or with friends, and couldn't bear to have the boat sit idle because I couldn't take it out.

In any marriage there is a push-pull of independence and dependence. My independence has always been important to me, so mastering the boat was only a matter of time. Sometimes it frightens me how dependent Jeff and I really are on each other, and I have long joked with him that I want to be the one to die first. It's not really a joke, although the reasoning behind it has shifted as we've gotten older. Without Jeff, I would remain alone. No one could measure up or take his place, although I like the company of people most of the time. We were so desperately in love in the first years of our marriage, I couldn't imagine that my life without him would be worth living. I still feel the same, but now would have the added problems of trying to figure out the remotes to the TV, opening a pickle jar, or doing the myriad mechanical chores that he performs effortlessly to maintain the house.

He's dependent on me, too. In addition to providing him the intimacy and deep connection that a good marriage affords, I help him with his wardrobe, saving him the embarrassment of going out in public looking like a jackass. I'm the main gift buyer, and the primary communicator with the children, translating his silences into the love and support he feels but can't always express. By choice and because of a vast skill differential, I am the primary cook, so I feed Jeff most of his meals. Although Jeff eats to survive if I am not available to cook, I prepare the family meals, the holiday meals, and almost everything in between. I enjoy it, and like it that he is dependent on me for his very sustenance. Secretly, I relish knowing I have control of my family's food, and I keep my olive oil in a beautiful old cobalt-blue bottle. My stepdaughter found the bottle and encouraged me to get it. It has an old glass stopper, and a faded label that reads "arsenic." The label is harder to read as the bottle gets oilier, but I know it's there.

The fact that my driving the boat meant that I was driving *his dad's* boat added an extra layer to my trepidations. The boat was so important to Jeff in both real and sentimental ways. That he let me, *encouraged me*, to drive it, is a testament to his selflessness, although things went better when he wasn't actually in the boat with me.

In the end, despite the braking issue, driving a boat *is* just like driving a car. It's like learning to ride a bike. At some point, you have to just get on and go. Once you have a familiarity with the mechanics of the thing, it's about guts and determination. I waited until I was alone to give it a try.

It was a sunny morning and the lake was calm when I decided to give the boat a go. Jeff was in Delaware. The girls were with me, but as usual were sleeping in. The lakefront was quiet as I snuck down to the dock, keys in one hand and a backpack with a towel, book, and bottle of water in the other. I turned the switch to begin lowering the lift, and unsnapped the cover from the boat, working my way around the outside, then the inside. I removed the metal bars that hold the cover up, then folded it into a big wad of canvas that I stuffed into the storage area under the bow. I climbed out of the boat to finish lowering the lift, and when the boat moved freely in the water, climbed back in and settled into the driver's seat. My hands were sweaty, my stomach had butterflies, and I felt generally shaky as I inserted the key into the slot and lowered the engine into the water. The engine caught. I looked carefully around, fiddled with the throttle until I remembered how to put the boat in reverse, and backed out. After I cleared the dock, I slowly edged the boat forward and tried to ignore my beating heart as I moved into open water.

I practiced driving, pushing the throttle to go faster and pulling back on it to slow down. I took wide turns, then tighter ones as I worked to keep my bearings. The lake looks very different on the water than it does from shore, but I had the big roof of Midway and the Institution bell tower as my landmarks, my watermarks. I puttered along the shoreline for a time, and then decided to drop the anchor and relax in the boat for a bit. I slowed down, then threw the boat into reverse to stop, lowered the anchor, shut off the motor, and stretched out on one of the back seats to sun and read. I tried to relax, but was too restless to focus on the book. I could hear other boats on the water, and although the boat was firmly anchored, it was far from still. The floating, so restful when I was in the boat with Jeff, was a little unnerving out there all by myself. After a while I pulled up the anchor and headed for home.

My stomach knotted up again as I neared our place. I had to concentrate to spot our dock in the middle of all the others as I planned how and when I would make the turns to slip the boat back into the lift. I rounded the bend and saw all sorts of people on the lawn in front; I would have an audience for my first solo landing. I passed the dock, turned the boat around, aimed, and pulled into the lift as if I'd done it all my life.

Clapping and cheering, Butch, Spike, and Emil all ran over to help me with the lift.

"I saw you over by Midway," Emil said. "I was going to stop, thought you were in trouble, but then I saw your head."

"I was just trying to read," I said.

Although Jeff showed me how the boat worked, Spike Kelderhouse really taught me to drive it. Every time I took it out, Spike, or sometimes Butch and Spike, would be there on the lakefront to watch me pull into the lift. They always seemed to know where I'd been. At first I thought Spike was just watching out for Jeff's boat. Because he was so grizzled and such a salty dog, I figured he didn't take to women in boats. I was surprised that he was truly supportive and encouraging. I knew he'd run a charter fishing business for years. Later, I learned that his wife, Norma, was a full partner, and as skilled with boats and knowledgeable of lake lore as he was.

If I did well, the old guys on the lakefront would cheer me on, and if I didn't, Spike would dispense just the advice I needed.

"When it's windy like this, you have to give it a little more gas," he said. "You have to have more power than the wind." Or, "Bring it around a little farther, and then you won't have to make such a tight turn to get it in the lift."

Once when I pulled in after it started raining, Spike was there.

"It's okay to stay out during a light rain like this," he said, and then he pointed toward the northwest. "But when you see a storm blowing in from Lake Erie, you come home. If the sky starts turning black over there, you bring her in fast. The lake can be dangerous."

Now I drive the boat all the time. I've taken kids and friends out to ride around, to ski and tube, to swim and float, and to restaurant destinations. There's nothing better than tooling down the lake with the sun and wind in your face headed for the Village Casino in Bemus, and nothing more fun than nailing the landing back at the dock. I still get the jitters, especially the first time I take the boat out in the season, but I face my fears and do it anyway. It helps me appreciate the ground after being a little unmoored, slightly unanchored.

~

During our second full season as owners, Saturday afternoon of the long Fourth of July weekend was cloudy and windy; the water was choppy and gray. The sun broke through occasionally and warmed us up, but we wore sweatshirts and jackets on the lakefront. Jeff hadn't fished that morning because it was so rough, but there were many boats on the lake since it was a holiday weekend. George Whitbeck was on the lakeside road talking to a neighbor who lived down toward Midway, and walked over when he was finished. Spike saw George walking toward us and tagged along.

"Tom McClain heard on his scanner that somebody drowned over by the Institution. The sheriff's got the boat out looking for the body, and if they don't find it by tonight, they're going to start dredging," George said.

"Oh, geez," Jeff said. "What happened?"

"I guess it was a young kid, twenty or so. He was out in a boat with his girlfriend and her family. A little girl who was with them was in the water, swimming, and started floating away. Apparently the kid jumped in to save her, and he got her back to the boat. But then he went down when a wave went over his head."

"If they don't find him, he'll show up here," Spike said. "Yup, this is where the body will end up. Right here in Maple Springs. If he went over in the middle of the lake, out that way in front of the Institution, the current will bring him in right here. This is where the bodies end up. Right here."

Jeff and I spent most of the rest of that day on the lakefront, sitting in the chairs sipping coffee, quietly talking. We'd go inside and putter around, and we tried to nap, but we couldn't settle in. I tried not to, but I couldn't help thinking about what had happened. Did they see that boy actually go under the water? How long did they stay out there in that boat, calling his name, before their voices gave out and they gave up? Exactly when did they start the boat and head toward shore? We all live on a lake, and swim. I thought about what that moment must be like when you can't swim anymore; when you just stop swimming.

The news of the drowning spread through the community quickly, and people came down to the lakefront in groups, or by ones and twos, to learn more or to talk it out. They sat quietly and watched the water, as if plumbing its mysteries and depths. The lake seemed different, unfathomable, having swallowed a boy's body but not yet released it.

The talk, the questions, went on into the evening.

"Didn't he have on a lifejacket? . . . No one should be out on the water on a day like this, let alone *in* the water . . . must have been tourists . . . I'm not going swimming until they find the body! . . . How old was that little girl? . . . From Jamestown, I heard . . . How far out were they? . . . The baby had on a life-jacket, but that boy didn't . . . Crying shame . . ."

It was the old men who took the news in and held it deep. They felt the weight, the gravity, of it. Doc Cummiskey had a worried look on his face and hung his head. Butch sat down hard in one of the metal chairs, but all he said was "Oh," in a low, sad tone. I could see the accumulated losses of their lifetimes wash across their faces. Their own long lives gave them a better sense of the meaning of what is lost when a young man drowns. They'd seen it before: what can happen when the water is too rough, or too deep.

For almost a week there was a pall over the lake. Not many boats were on the water, and the kids refused to swim. Jeff didn't fish.

"Fishermen don't like to fish when there's a body in the water," he said.

Although we had the usual fireworks and flares, the Fourth of July celebration was muted. It was as though the whole community was holding its breath. We all tried to go on as usual, but everyone was watching, out of the corners of their eyes, for the body.

After the Fourth, Jeff had to go back to work in Delaware. I decided to stay on for a few more days with the girls. That summer, Kayla was the odd man out, and she hung out with me while the two older girls conspired to find boys. Kayla separated her Midway money into a daily allowance. I walked her down every morning so she could spend it playing skeeball—she had her eye on a stuffed dog and wanted to earn enough tickets to get it before the trip ended. By midweek, she begged me to let her go alone, and I nervously acquiesced as long as she promised to go straight there and come straight home. After a couple of days I relaxed a bit. She was almost twelve, and it was Maple Springs, so I figured it was safe. But the body in the lake made everything seem dangerous that summer. I wanted to keep my own chicks close.

On Thursday morning I woke early to voices on the lakefront. I turned over to try to get some more sleep, but when the voices persisted, I got up to take a look. I opened the sliding glass door on the upstairs balcony and saw the Chautauqua County coroner's van parked on the lawn. Despite the commotion, I hadn't realized what was going on until I saw the van. Jesse Kelderhouse was there, talking to one of the EMTs.

All sorts of things went through my mind as what I was witnessing slowly registered. The body was there, right out front. I hadn't put my glasses on, so was straining to see. At the same time, I was repulsed and didn't want to see anything. The girls were all sleeping in the other room. Of course, they'd been saddened by the death and had worried about the body all week. I thought to wake them, in part because it felt I was a lonely, singular witness to the horror and, in part, because I knew they would want to be in on the action. I thought about what I would tell them when they did wake. What did a body that had been in a lake for a week look like? I was repulsed, but at the same time I was drawn to the scene and felt compelled to witness it. I quickly turned away, grabbed my glasses, went downstairs, and put on the coffee.

By the time I came out with coffee for Jesse, the event was over.

"I put cream in, wasn't sure how you take it," I said to Jesse. "Wanna come sit on the porch?"

We settled in, and Jesse talked for a long time. He was pretty shaken up. "I was walking on the lakefront road about six o'clock," he said. "I looked out at the lake and saw something sticking out of the water." Jesse took a slow sip of coffee and scanned the lake. "It was two hands."

"Your dad said the body would end up here," I said.

"I went over to the Strah's house down the street and called the police," he said. "The lights were all out at the townhouses. By the time I got back, the cops were here and the body was under your dock." He sat quietly for a long time.

"This isn't the first body I've found down here," he said. Jesse, a stunned look on his face, began to relax a little. "The currents pull everything this way. Not just dead fish."

After Jesse left, I called Jeff in his office in Delaware.

"They found the body," I said. "It was under our dock. The girls are still sleeping. Come up as soon as you can . . ."

Spike

spike: n. a sharp momentary increase in voltage or electrical current; a transient variation in voltage or current.

By August, when Jeff and I drove up again for a long weekend by ourselves, the shock of the drowning had waned. The big news was Spike Kelderhouse turning eighty, and the Kelderhouse kids, now men and women in their forties and fifties, organized a party, inviting the whole neighborhood. When we arrived, there were tents, shelters, picnic tables, and grills set up in front of the shuffleboard, and some of the Kelderhouses were already there, in campers.

Spike and his first wife, Norma, had eight children: two girls and six boys. All the kids were given names that started with the letters *JE*. Jean and Jeryl are the girls. The boys are named Jerry, Jed, Jevin, Jeff, Jesse, and Jerrett; everyone calls Jerrett, the youngest son, Pete. The Kelderhouses were prolific, and after a while the neighbors, upon hearing of another arrival of a new JE-something Kelderhouse, would exclaim, "JEsus! Not another one!"

By the time we got to the party, it was in full swing. All sorts of people showed up: neighbors we knew and those we hadn't yet met, friends from around the lake, and Kelderhouse relations from as far away as West Virginia and Florida.

Spike was, of course, the center of attention. Along with his corncob pipe and big grin, he was wearing a T-shirt, a hat he got from Jeff with Jeff's business logo prominently displayed, and a pair of ghetto shorts. Spike called them clamdiggers. In those shorts, Spike looked like a Popeye version of Warren Beatty, when he lost his mind in *Bulworth* and was running around with Halle Berry.

Butch and Marge were there, along with other townhouse neighbors, and Tom Cummiskey, the doctor who lived in the big house on the circle. Butch and Spike usually celebrated their birthdays together. Butch was younger than Spike by five years and five days. But this landmark day was exclusively Spike's. The townhouse residents had chipped in to get him his own chair for the lakefront. Jeff and I picked it up at an Amish place we drove past on our way to the lake from Delaware, and we'd had a plaque made for it that read, "This is Spike's Chair," along with the date.

"Look at this chair that the condo people got me," Spike said to whoever would listen. Then he'd stand up, show them the plaque, and dive back into the conversation.

The Kelderhouse kids were all there, too. We met the girls, who were well-muscled, but tiny. The boys were all variations of Spike: big, blonde, and balding, with powerful, muscular builds. Jed was a serious-looking version of Spike, and Jeff Kelderhouse looked like a jolly Spike, with bright blue eyes that crinkled when he laughed. Jesse, Jevin, and Pete all resembled their father, and they all resembled each other. Jesse had legs like tree trunks. Although most people moved the docks and boatlifts around with ATVs and tractors, Jesse sometimes just stuffed himself into a tight wetsuit and wrestled them into the back of a rowboat, unassisted.

The Kelderhouse guys, heavy or slim, all have a certain mass to them, a heft.

The Kelderhouses were experienced, robust picnickers. For the party, two or three big tables were loaded with side dishes and desserts. They cooked chicken, steaks, and burgers on several grills: regular grills along with half-barrels retrofitted with grates, filled with charcoal.

I sat down next to Doc Cummiskey to eat. A couple of the Kelderhouse sons walked through the crowd offering grilled corn, still in the husk, with another Kelderhouse behind holding a coffee can filled with melted butter for dunking. The crowd was noisy, so Doc and I settled in for some serious eating and gossiping. He and I had become friends after I helped him pick out new wallpaper for his cottage.

"Do you know all these people?" I asked him. "I can't believe how many Kelderhouses there are."

"I've met them all over the years," he replied. "Jean and Pete Kelderhouse both live out west, so they don't make it back very often. The rest of them live around here, so I see them occasionally. Jesse's here all the time, and you know Jevin, don't you? He keeps his boat, that white cabin cruiser, on the buoy."

"I've seen him, but never met him," I said.

"Jerry's not here," Doc continued. "Nobody has seen him for a long time. I'm not sure if anyone knows where he is." Doc took a sip of bourbon, and looked at me seriously, but with a twinkle in his eye. "He's among the missing."

"What happened?" I asked.

"Rumor has it," Doc said, "that he had a predilection for women's clothing. I think he was caught dressing up in them."

"Poor thing," I said, imagining the reaction of the family and the neighborhood. "That would be difficult, given what the rest of these guys and their dad are like."

"Yes, I imagine it would be," Doc said with a sigh. Doc himself had never married, and rumors swirled about his sexuality, too. He spoke occasionally of a long-ago broken engagement with an heiress, but what, or who, kept him going for the last fifty years of his life was a mystery.

The party continued well into the evening. Even after we went to bed, Jeff and I could hear laughter coming from the shuffleboard and the lakefront. It was almost midnight when they started in with the fireworks.

The next day all the Kelderhouse guys went swimming off their dock. They started out doing cannonballs and such, and then went into a comic synchronized swimming routine, carefully holding their beers out of the water. I called Jeff to come watch.

Jeff watched a while with his mouth hanging open, then laughed. "I bet they were hilarious as kids. Like a bunch of overgrown puppies."

We watched until they ended their swim and climbed onto the dock. Still laughing, they walked back to their property in a group, all of them in cut-offs or shorts, Jesse in the lead and Pete bringing up the rear.

"Oh, my God," I said to Jeff. "I think I can feel the ground shake. That's a lot of beef coming down the road."

Jeff just stared and shook his head. "Yup," he said. "That's a lot of beef."

∽

The summer after his birthday party, Spike was slowing down, and sick. He was pale and his ankles were painfully swollen. Occasionally his wife would drive him down to watch the sunset and check on his boats, but he couldn't always get out of the car. His trips to the lakefront grew irregular and finally stopped altogether. We missed the sound of his voice on the lakefront, and realized how integral it had been as a background for all of our experiences. That October, he died.

Doc Cummiskey thought that Spike had leukemia or some other sort of blood disorder. "He looked so awful, so pale, the last time I saw him," he told me later. "I had to walk around the building so he couldn't see that I was crying. I knew it would be the last time I saw him."

A picture of Spike from the birthday party, with the corncob pipe and wearing Jeff's company hat, was front and center in the big photographic display the Kelderhouses put together for Spike's funeral service. The photo was surrounded by many others: Spike as a young man, Spike with fish, Spike on boats. Spike in a military uniform. Spike surrounded by his wife and children when the children were small, in front of the hotel.

The service at the Lutheran church was packed. All the Kelderhouses showed up except Jean and Jerry. Jeff and I drove from Delaware to pay our respects and say goodbye. The O'Connors and Tom Cummiskey arrived from Buffalo.

Normally, fall is our favorite time of year at the lake. The turning leaves light up the lakeshore and the surrounding hills, most of the summer residents are gone, and we can spend peaceful time outside during warm Indian summer days and nights. But we were sad to lose our friend, sad to lose what Spike represented of the lake. Losing Spike meant losing the vast history of the lake that he both forged and carried with him. It meant losing his steward-ship. Spike didn't wait for permission, or for a committee, to take care of the lake and the lakefront. He planted things, buried dead fish, picked up sticks, dispensed advice, and enforced the unwritten rules. He was the keeper of the flame. Even though we hadn't been at the lake that long, we felt the sting of a deep loss.

We milled around in the narthex waiting for the services to begin, looking at the pictures and quietly talking. Jesse Kelderhouse gave me a big hug, let loose for a minute, and gave me a big hug all over again. He was dressed in a sport coat and long khaki pants, almost unrecognizable from his usual lakefront attire, and his eyes were red-rimmed from crying. His brushy hair stuck up around his bald spots.

The minister delivered a solid eulogy. He'd obviously known Spike. I doubted that Spike was a Sunday regular, at least during fishing season, which, depending on what one is fishing for, is all year long. The basic theme was about Spike's being a character, and what a fixture he was on the lake. When the minister was finished, he invited the funeral-goers to speak if they had something they wanted to say about Spike.

Spike's son Jed stood up to speak for the family.

"Thank you all for coming," he began. "You all know what a character my dad was. But I think the best thing about him was that he was a great teacher." Jed's voice cracked as he choked up. Jeff Kelderhouse stood up and put an arm around his brother's shoulder. Jed couldn't continue, thanked everyone for coming again, and sat back down.

Several people stood and reminisced about when they'd met Spike and how long they'd known him and the rest of the family. Someone had gone to high school with him. They talked about how the lake wouldn't be the same without Spike. A fisherman named Lanny, a regular on the lakefront, told a story about getting caught in a violent storm on the lake and taking shelter under a bridge until it passed.

"Spike pulled up in his old pickup and found me," he said. "He was worried, and knew right where I'd be." Lanny got all choked up, too.

Tom Cummiskey stood up and slowly made his way to the front of the church. He climbed the stairs, took his place behind the lectern, and adjusted his tie.

"My name is Tom Cummiskey," he said with great precision. "I met Spike not long after I bought my cottage. It's been, let's see, almost twenty-five years ago now. I was looking for someone to help me with maintenance, and heard that Spike helped people with chores on the lake. I called Spike's number on several occasions, and left messages. But I never heard back from him. I finally tracked him down on the lakefront.

"I introduced myself, and explained to Spike that I'd recently purchased the cottage and was looking for someone to help me cut the grass, winterize, and watch over the place if I wasn't there.

"In his characteristic way," Doc continued, "Spike started chatting. 'Yes, you've come to the right man,' he said. 'I do all sorts of work around here. You could say I manage the lake.'

"He welcomed me to the neighborhood, and asked where I was from. I told him I was from Buffalo," Doc said. "Williamsville, actually. I told him that I'd called his number several times and left messages for him to call back. But my calls were not returned.

"Spike told me he was busy, and in high demand. 'I don't return phone calls,' he said. 'I'm just like a doctor, just like a doctor.' We finished talking about what I needed to have done, and then Spike asked, 'And what do you do, Tom?' "

Doc paused for a minute, for effect and to pull himself together. " 'I'm a doctor,' I said."

Doc laughed, took a deep breath, and said, "I'm going to miss his friendship. I'm really going to miss him." Turning to the pews filled with Kelderhouses, he continued, "I am very sorry for your loss."

Spike was buried at the lovely old cemetery in Bemus Point. The cemetery is beautifully landscaped with roses, tree hydrangeas, and huge rhododendrons, and overlooks the water. He still has a view of the lake. Jeff and I visited the grave together once, and Jeff goes over occasionally by himself. He talks to Spike. He seeks Spike's counsel when there is a difficulty or dispute on the lakefront, and catches him up on the news.

Summer of Changes

Then summer fades and passes and October comes. We'll smell smoke then, and feel an unexpected sharpness, a thrill of nervousness, swift elation, a sense of sadness and departure.

—Thomas Wolfe

Jeff and I returned to the lake in May the year after Spike died to get the boat in the water. After some unseasonably warm spring weather, the cold returned. On Mother's Day weekend, when I usually plant my deck and container flowers, it snowed hard little pellets that seemed more like Styrofoam than snow. A bitter wind stirred up the waves and washed newly installed dock sections down the lake.

Butch and Marge arrived from Florida, dismayed that it was still so cold at Chautauqua. We went outside to hug them, and to help them unload their van.

"It's cold!" Butch said, shivering. "Let's ride out this weather, and why not join us for happy hour on Friday. This cold can't last forever." Spike's absence was palpable, and unloading their van in the frigid cold made their getting settled for the season even more difficult.

The next morning was still cold when the lakefront exploded with swallows. Swooping and diving for invisible bugs that were newly hatched, or maybe blown shoreward by the wind, the swallows whirled and whipped, rose and fell. I called Jeff over to look.

"Wow," he said. "It's like a tornado, or being inside a blender." The swallows swirled in and out of our view. They pivoted and spun in the air, their forked tails acting like dual control rudders. The next day the weather cleared and they were gone, leaving the lakefront to the less acrobatic birds: the orioles, cardinals, sparrows, and wrens.

The summer after Spike died was lonesome, especially for Butch. Spike had been Butch's constant companion. Although Butch had golfing buddies and socialized with other neighbors when they were around, he and Spike chatted daily and almost always had a project they were working on. They messed around in the pump room, worked on boats, painted the metal chairs we all used at the fire pit, planted the gardens, shared the news.

Jeff and I had kids who were getting bigger, and who had summer obligations with work and friends. Between their schedules and our work schedules, our time at the lake was limited. Our absence made Butch and Marge even lonelier. Before long, they started talking about selling.

Butch and Marge were among the first people we met when we bought the townhouse, and over the years our friendship had deepened. They had welcomed us unreservedly as neighbors, introduced us to their friends and acquaintances, and schooled us in lake lore and neighborhood gossip. They were genuinely happy with our accomplishments, and understanding of our failures.

In 2001, after the awful events of 9/11, Jeff and I drove up to the lake. We sat quietly with Butch and Marge on the lakefront, marveling at the stars. We watched them twinkle and shoot.

"You don't realize how many planes are in the sky here, until there aren't any," said Marge.

It was a comfort to us to be at the lake then, with our good friends, during that sad, sad time.

Jeff and Butch did chores together. They sealed the parking lot with Mike O'Connor, and fixed each other's boats. Jeff would start on something, and Butch would appear with a wrench, or just support and advice. Butch and Marge were part of the rhythm of our life at the lake, and we couldn't imagine being there without them.

One morning we got up early to have breakfast out and run some errands. We were unloading groceries when Mary Ferris walked over. She and her husband, Joe, a doctor from Erie, lived on the circle next door to Doc Cummiskey.

"We just took Butch to the hospital," she said.

"Is he okay?" we asked.

"I'm not sure what's going on yet," she said. "He was having terrible stomach pains. Marge called me, and I helped get him to the couch and sat with them until the ambulance came. Joe thinks it might be a blockage, or his pancreas."

Later in the evening, Doc Cummiskey came over and sat on the porch with us. "I spoke with Butch's doctor," he said. "It's not cancer. He's had an attack of pancreatitis. Generally it resolves itself, so he should be fine. It's very painful, though."

"What causes it?" I asked.

"Gallstones. Or alcoholism," Doc said. "They've ruled out gallstones."

"Butch isn't an alcoholic," I said. "He drinks at happy hour, but never more than two."

"Lately he's been having a Guinness every day," Jeff said. "For medicinal purposes. He read in *Prevention Magazine* that it's good for you."

"No, Butch isn't an alcoholic," Doc said as he sipped his bourbon. "Sometimes it's idiopathic."

"What does idiopathic mean?" I asked.

Doc laughed. "It means we don't know what caused it. That we're idiots."

All week we waited for updates from Marge on Butch's condition. Their daughter Bonnie came up from Ohio, and Marge discouraged us from visiting. The two of them went up to the hospital every day. By the end of the week, Marge was dragging. Butch's "spell" scared her; it was difficult for her to see him in pain, and difficult for her to think about his mortality, especially so soon after Spike died. I called her on Thursday to ask them to join us for dinner, and invited Doc Cummiskey, too.

We sat and talked over pork tenderloin that I marinated in peanut oil, garlic, chili powder, and lime juice, then grilled. Doc brought his own bottle of bourbon, and got up several times to refill his glass. Marge caught us up on Butch's progress. "I think they're going to release him in a few days," she said. "But he's weak."

Things were fine until Doc shifted the conversation to politics.

"I've changed my party affiliation to Democrat," he said. "I've been a Republican all my life, but I've had it with George Bush."

He continued, even though I was giving him looks meant to signal that he should shut up. Marge was short on patience since she was tired and worried about Butch, and I could see her getting more agitated.

"What would you have him do with all these terrorists running around?" she asked, her voice becoming shrill.

"I was supportive of going into Afghanistan," Doc said. "There was a clear connection between the attack on the Twin Towers and Al Qaida. But I can't support going into Iraq. There are no weapons of mass destruction! Bush lied to us!"

Marge stood up with a huff. "I'm leaving," she said. She stopped on her way to the door and turned back to Doc. "George Bush is just like Jesus Christ!" she said. "He's persecuted!"

"I guess I should go, too," Bonnie, her daughter, said. She was uncomfortable, and so was everybody else. Jeff hadn't said anything, but his eyebrows were going ninety miles an hour.

"Did I go too far?" Doc asked after they left. "Do *you* think there were weapons of mass destruction?"

"I think we shouldn't talk about politics at the lake," I said. "Marge is tired, and stressed out. And so am I. We can talk more tomorrow."

The next morning the phone started ringing early. I listened to Marge and Doc rail on about one another, about George Bush, and about George Bush detractors. "Yes, you should apologize to her," I told Doc. "You've been friends for a very long time. She was already upset about Butch." "He didn't mean for you to take it personally," I said to Marge. "He shouldn't have started in on politics at all, and definitely not after so much bourbon. You should forget it, you've been friends for a very long time."

Just when I was finally getting into the shower, the phone rang again. It was Marge. "They're letting Butch out of the hospital this morning," she said.

I asked if she wanted us to go with her, or if there was anything we could do, but she said no.

When I got out of the shower, Jeff told me Marge had called again. "She said she's not ready, and wanted to know if we could go get Butch. I told her yes. C'mon."

When we got to the hospital, Butch was sitting up on the side of his bed. His eyes welled up when he saw us. Jeff and I carried his things while they wheeled him down to the car.

"I'm glad to be out of that place," he said. "Thanks for coming to get me." He stared out the window the whole way home, taking stock of the sky and the scenery. "I'm glad I'm alive," he said, and his eyes welled up again.

Butch recovered slowly, but he soon began making his way outside. He quit drinking, even though drinking hadn't caused his problem. "I don't want to risk it," he said. "That pancreatitis hurt!"

Butch's health problems firmed their resolve to sell their place, and they found a buyer in the middle of the summer.

"We're not closing until after Labor Day," Marge told us.

"We're going to miss you," Jeff said.

"Are you sure you want to go?" I asked.

"We've told each other for a long time that we'd know when it was time to sell," Marge said. "It's time. I'm getting tired of the long drive twice a year, and Butch is lonely without Spike. A lot of our friends up here are gone now. But we'll see you again."

~

After Spike died, the lot, equipment, and shuffleboard and all its contents were deeded to the kids in an eight-way split. The division of the property did not go smoothly. There were shouting matches between various Kelderhouse brothers on the lot, and more than once, fists flew. They sold Spike's old, green John Deere tractor, even though Jesse used it regularly for his work with the docks and lifts. Despite the fussing, the Kelderhouses had a renewed commitment to keep the family together after Spike was gone, and decided to throw a party over the Fourth of July. Jeff Kelderhouse stopped over and invited us. "Bring something to grill," he said. "And a side dish, if you want."

Just as they did for Spike's birthday party, the Kelderhouse kids set up picnic tables under tents and shelters. The tables were loaded with food. RVs and campers, full of Kelderhouses and their relations, were parked on the perimeter of their lot, and several grills were set on low heat for chicken, or on high for steaks. Doc Cummiskey was there, along with several other neighbors, but Jeff and I were the only ones from the townhouses in attendance. Later I found out we were the only ones from the townhouses to be invited.

I love to cook, and along with chicken to grill, had brought parsleyed new potatoes and a big fruit salad.

"My mom used to make these potatoes," Jesse Kelderhouse said. "Lots of butter and parsley. These are great."

Jed Kelderhouse devoured the fruit salad. I make it with a little sugar and some fruit-flavored vinegar, white balsamic flavored with figs, or pears. The vinegar brings out the flavors and keeps the fruit. "Can I have seconds?" Jed asked, and when I nodded yes, he looked over at his brother Jeff. "Look at this. Kiwi, and raspberries. And what's this? Mangoes?"

While we ate and visited, people walking by on the lakeside road stopped over for a chat. Many offered their condolences to the kids over Spike's death. Even if their experiences at Chautauqua were brief, or had happened long ago, almost everyone seemed to have known Spike.

Jeff Kelderhouse got up and headed toward one of the grills. Barefoot and bare chested, he'd been slow-cooking chicken for almost an hour.

"Did you guys live in the hotel?" my Jeff asked.

"We did in the summertime, when we were older," Jesse said. He laughed and took a swig of beer. "We were the hired help!"

"The rest of the time, we lived in that house," Jed said, pointing behind him. "The one where the Ruhs live now. The land was part of the hotel property, and my dad built the house in 1962."

Jeff Kelderhouse put a big platter of chicken down in the middle of the table. "Have some," he said.

Even though we'd finished our meal a while ago, I took a piece.

"Oh, my God," I said. "How did you do this chicken? It's the best grilled chicken I've ever had."

"Marinated it in Chiavetta's," Jeff said. "Then cooked it slow."

Chiavetta's is a local marinade, a vinegar-and-oil-based barbecue sauce that is wonderful for enhancing the flavor and texture of grilled chicken. It's good on pork, too. I'd never heard of it, even though I'd discovered and enjoyed other local products, like Weber's horseradish mustard, and that divine maple cream. Now friends and family from all over the country are fans.

I regularly brought the Chiavetta's, the mustard, cheese, and some of the local produce home so we could enjoy them when we weren't at the lake. But I never brought the maple cream home, wanting instead to reserve it for enjoying only when we were at the lake. To me, it's as integral to the place, as organic, as the view of the lake itself, and could truly be savored only on site.

"I've never been in the Ruh's house," said my Jeff. "It doesn't look big enough for all of you from the outside."

"It's got four bedrooms," Jed said. "Mom and Dad had one, the girls had one, and we had one for the big boys and one for the little boys."

"Your mom must have had her hands full," I said.

"She did! She did!" Jeff Kelderhouse said. "But we didn't get into too much trouble. We could have gone to jail, but we didn't. Sometimes the cops brought us home, but we knew if we ended up in jail, we weren't getting bailed out."

"Remember that time that Jerry shot out the window?" Jed asked.

"Mom and Dad never found out about that," said Jesse.

Jeff Kelderhouse told the story. It was hunting season, and the boys had a bunch of loaded guns propped up in a corner of their bedroom. "Jerry came home late one night, all drunk," he said. "And he kicked over the guns, and fired off three shots. One went clean through my pillow!"

"We snuck back in the house the next afternoon," Jed said. "Jerry and I fixed the window and moved a dresser in front of a hole in the wall. I can't believe we never got caught."

The afternoon was growing late and the crowd had thinned to the Kelderhouses, a few of their close friends, and us. It felt nice, warm, and intimate to hear them talk and reminisce. Both Jeff and I felt honored to be included.

"My dad would have been happy with this party," Jeff Kelderhouse said. He started to tear up. "We've all had some great times on the lake. I'd like to hear other people's stories about their summers at the lake." He glanced at us, and continued. "Even if you didn't spend summers here, you could tell a story about your own family vacations, or other lakes you've been to."

The stories started swirling: about fish, about swimming across the lake, about staying in Grandma's cottage. My Jeff talked about vacations he spent with his parents on Lake George, Lake Champlain, Speculator Lake. Although Jeff's parents were only marginally middle class, they always took family vacations.

I sat there mute and stunned, trying to think of something I could say to skip my turn. I couldn't remember a single vacation my family took, never mind anything about a lake vacation. I struggled to remember a good time, but I couldn't. Usually I'm comfortable being pretty open about my bad childhood, but in this context of nostalgia and peaceful remembrances, I wasn't. Caught off guard, my mind reeled in my panic. I sat very still until it was blissfully time to depart.

Jeff put his hand on my shoulder as we walked the short distance home. "You got a raw deal," he said.

"It's okay," I said. "But thanks for saying it." Even though I don't spend a lot of time talking about my childhood, Jeff has been around long enough to understand. "It really wasn't that bad. I just couldn't think of anything to say."

"It was that bad," he said. "Yes, it was."

∽

We didn't make it back to the lake until Labor Day that year. The usual gang, Emil and Betty, the O'Connors, the Whitbecks, and many other neighbors were there for the party, but the tone was subdued. It was Butch and Marge's last Labor Day with us. Butch made his fabulous chocolate rum cake, and I made grilled shrimp with a cucumber salsa.

The weekend was warm, but fall was in the air. We felt it when the wind blew a certain way, and occasionally a maple tree dropped a brilliant leaf, a sure sign of change. A lot of the seasonal people, especially those with kids, were starting to shut down their cottages and would not return until spring.

"You cry with joy when people leave at the end of the season because you're so sick of 'em, you're glad to see 'em go," Jesse Kelderhouse told us one day as he was describing what it's like to live at the lake all year round. "Then you cry in the spring, because you're so glad to see 'em come back!" But that Labor Day was especially sad for us because Butch and Marge were leaving.

The day after the party, Jeff and I were catching up on outside chores. I was outside weeding the garden when I heard, then saw, Jeff Kelderhouse's big diesel truck pull down the lakeside road. I waved at him, and then hollered, "Hey, Jeff. How you doing?"

"Okay," he said. "Just down for the day helping with the dock. We lost a couple of sections in the storm last week."

"Wanna eat?" I asked.

"Sure," he said without hesitation, although he'd never been to our place for dinner before. "What time?"

Jeff showed up at the designated time, and we had a nice visit and a good dinner. We caught up on family, and the Jeffs—my Jeff and Jeff Kelderhouse—talked about the fact that the wells that supply water to the townhouses are the same wells that supplied the hotel. "There's an old discharge pipe still in the water," Jeff K said.

"I've seen it," my Jeff said. "I can't believe they ran the waste water right into the lake."

"When we were kids," Jeff K responded, "we didn't swim off Midway. The water was totally brown there. And stinky."

My Jeff asked why they tore down the Whiteside Hotel.

"The town was running sewer lines," Jeff K said. "And wanted to enforce sprinkler codes. We just couldn't afford to retrofit an old wooden hotel. The season is so short up here, it's hard to make a go of it, even in good years."

"How come they call your brother Pete?" I asked.

"Well, his name's Jerrett, you know," said Jeff K. "All of us have names that start with JE. But one day when he was a little kid, my dad looked at him and said, 'You look like a Pete.' And the name stuck."

"How did Spike get his name?" my Jeff asked.

"Well, his name is Donald. But one day when he was a little kid, his dad was working on something and had some big spikes lying around. He told my dad not to touch the spikes. My dad must have liked the word or something, he started saying 'Spike spike spike spike spike.' So they started calling him Spike, and it stuck. For eighty years!"

Jeff K stuck a toothpick in his mouth, leaned back in his chair, and looked out the sliding door at the lake. "You've got a great view of your boat from here," he said. "I like that boat. It's got good attitude."

I knew what he was talking about. Jesse Kelderhouse had said the same thing about our boat, and so had Spike. Attitude refers to how the boat sits on the water; how it moves through the water.

"Those old boats had good lines," he continued. "The chine and the hull . . . They don't make them like that anymore."

"What's a chine?" I interrupted, sitting up straighter in my chair. "I've never heard that lovely word before!"

"Oh, you like that?" Jeff K said, then he rattled off a bunch of other boat terms: transoms, gunnels, stringers, fairing. He laughed because he knew he was showing off. "The chine is where the bottom of the boat is attached to the sides. You can have hard chines or soft chines, or even double chines. Yours is nice, the way it looks and the way it cuts through the water." He laughed again, and leaned toward me playfully. "That's why it's got good *attitude*!"

He looked back outside. "You know, looking out at the lake from here is the same as looking out the front of the hotel. Yup, this is the same view. That tree there, that was here when the hotel was here. There was a foyer right here where we're sitting, with benches," he continued. "And over there," he said, pointing to his left, "that's where the dining room was."

"Is this the first time you've been in one of the townhouses?" my Jeff asked.

"Yes it is," Jeff K replied. "Yes it is."

It felt good to me to give Jeff Kelderhouse the gift of seeing the lake from the point of view of the hotel again. Truthfully, I was stunned that he'd never been in one of the townhouses after all these years. The Kelderhouses get a mixed review from the neighborhood. The newer people don't know their part in the history of this place, and others are a bit snobbish. Some people act like they own the place. They consider the Kelderhouses interlopers, even though the lake and almost all of the lakefront is community property and belongs to all of us.

Like any other place, people make judgments about others based on what they perceive as class, or money, or some other ascribed status. The reality is that there are all sorts of people in this little place, and what is perceived about them is as often wrong as it is right. There are some wealthy people who purchase or build vacation homes on the lake and use them seasonally. Other people inherit their cottages. Sometimes these cottages are simply used and abused until they're sold, the family unable or unwilling to pay taxes and upkeep bills. The people who live here full time represent a wide range of socioeconomic and educational backgrounds. Many people, like us, are working people who sacrificed other things to be in Maple Springs.

The Kelderhouse claim to this place is strong. They grew up here. They know the lake and are generous in sharing their knowledge. Despite their rough edges, both Jeff and I have a soft spot in our hearts for the Kelderhouses, and consider them our friends. Like their dad, the men work with their hands and their bodies. In today's America, working with one's hands is considered déclassé, but it's the only way to thrive here on the lake. It seems we're always pushing, pulling, lugging, towing, fixing, or shoveling something. Sometimes a Kelderhouse or two will offer to lend a hand, and we do the same in return. That's part of what knits our community. The Kelderhouses seem to accept us, too, based on our sensibilities about the lake, and nothing else.

After Labor Day, Jeff and I returned for another long weekend. We liked to celebrate my birthday at the lake, needed to pull the boat before the docks came out, and although we were dreading it, we had to say goodbye to Butch and Marge.

We joined Butch and Marge for dinner at the See-Zurh House in Bemus Point on Friday night. We'd never been; we'd avoided the place because the name was so stupid. Every time we passed it, one of the kids (or I) would say, "Let's go to the See-Zurh House and have a seizure." A lame joke, but it never failed to amuse us. Butch and Marge were regulars, so of course we agreed to join them.

The restaurant was crowded, but we found a table in the bar.

"There's another big dining room in the back," Marge said. "But we prefer eating out here. There's more action." She laughed, waving to Jesse Kelderhouse, who was sitting at the bar proper.

The restaurant is actually named after the two fellows who started it, Don See and Zurh Faulkner, but they apparently didn't get the seizure joke. The cover of the menu boasts "Live Entertainment Nightly . . . Just sit back and watch your fellow customers," and warns that "If you want fancy, this isn't the place!"

Butch and Marge ordered one steak sandwich to split, and the 24-ounce beer, one of the See-Zurh House specials. They split that, too. According to Butch, they always ordered the same thing, and always on Friday nights.

"We're going to miss this place," said Butch.

"We'll be back to visit," said Marge. "And you guys should come down to see us in Florida sometime."

We spent the rest of the evening gently reminiscing. It felt as if we'd known Butch and Marge for many more years than we had, and although they were our parents' ages, we'd become friends. Marge and I always laughed about something, and Butch was a gentle soul, always in a good mood, and always glad to see us. Perhaps because time seems compressed at the lake, or because of our growing awareness of how precious our time here is, it felt as if we had lived a lot of life alongside Butch and Marge.

Earlier that spring, my beloved grandfather had died at the age of ninety-one. My mother brought me some irises from his garden when she visited, the gnarly roots stuffed into her suitcase in plastic bags.

One morning, Butch helped me transplant them into my little lakefront garden.

"Just stick them in the ground," Butch said. "They'll grow."

He took my hand as we walked across the big front lawn, and it felt natural and fine. He coached me in the digging and knelt down to show me which way to plant the bulbs. He covered them gently with loose soil, his experienced gardener's hands working efficiently.

On our last day as neighbors, Butch knocked on the sliding glass door. "Is Jeff here?" he asked. Jeff went outside to chat.

"Butch wants me to take him out in the boat," he told me when they were finished.

They were gone for about an hour, but it wasn't until we got in bed that night that Jeff told me the story.

"Butch had a bunch of mementos he wanted to put in the lake," he said. "We went down by Long Point, and he dropped them in."

"What kind of mementos?" I asked.

"Things from his retirement," Jeff said. "A stainless steel plaque, a paperweight, and some sort of clock, I think. He said he didn't need them anymore, and he wanted something of himself to remain permanently in the lake."

My eyes filled with tears. "I'm really going to miss them. I'll always feel them up here," I said.

"They've been good friends," Jeff said. "They've taught us a lot about how to be an older couple. About how to be retired and live a good life. I like it that they split their sandwiches and beer."

I was quiet for a long time, thinking about losing Butch and Marge, mourning the losses that their advancing age was bringing them, and mourning my own loss at their going.

"We should do that," Jeff said. "That's how you live on less. Split your sandwich and your beer."

"They're still crazy about each other," I said.

"And they split their sandwiches and beer," Jeff said.

I think that Jeff was staving off his own feelings of loss by focusing on what he apparently thought was a brilliant financial tip, but I was getting annoyed at his ruining my reverie. "I don't care how old we get," I said. "Or how poor. I want my own fucking beer."

Barf Salad

When I walk into my kitchen today, I am not alone. Whether we know it or not, none of us is. We bring fathers and mothers and kitchen tables, and every meal we have ever eaten. Food is never just food. It's also a way of getting at something else: who we are, who we have been, and who we want to be.

—Molly Wizenberg *(A Homemade Life: Stories and Recipes from My Kitchen Table)*

I come from a long line of unexceptional cooks.

My maternal grandmother cooked all the time, but was a victim of a lack of talent, Lutheranism, a bland ethnic identity, and her generation: the generation introduced to convenience foods in the 1940s and '50s. The food she cooked and served was plain, usually consisting of overcooked meat—big meat, like ham and roast beef—and canned vegetables, or an occasional iceberg lettuce salad with bottled dressing.

When we were teenagers, she started experimenting with tacos, biscuit-crust pizza, and all manner of casseroles, from recipes she got from Junior League or church cookbooks. Most recipes contained some version of canned creamed soup: Campbell's cream of mushroom, chicken, tomato, or celery. Marshmallows and olives turned up unexpectedly in salads and casseroles, sometimes in hideous combinations that the TV chefs now call "sweet and savory." Canned oranges and jarred maraschino cherries made appearances along with the inevitable Cool Whip.

The food was abundant, however, and regularly served. Breakfast was simple: stacks of toast, coffee, bacon and eggs. We ate at the kitchen table, a draw leaf made of oak, with ends that pulled out and up to extend it. I learned to dunk buttery toast in my coffee from the milkman at Roberts Dairy, who regularly stopped in for a chat with my grandparents while on his route. Although Jeff thinks it's kind of gross, I still do it. It improves the taste of both the toast and the coffee. Meatloaf and spaghetti, Butter Brickle ice cream, Cheetos and chips stored in gigantic Tupperware containers, and big glass bottles of RC Cola in the cupboard under the telephone. Juicy Fruit chewing gum in the drawer with the Pall Malls.

My own mother was also an unremarkable cook, not from lack of talent, perhaps, but because of circumstances: too many kids born when she was too young. At twenty-five, she was already burdened with four children, an absurd and cataclysmic failure of both birth- and self-control. We ate food that could be stretched by macaroni or beans or both. We ate poor-people food, sometimes not enough, served with way too little happiness. Even today, you must ask to share my food before you grab it off my plate or risk being stabbed by my fork.

In between disastrous moves to Russellville, Arkansas; Norman, Oklahoma; Sunflower Village, Kansas; and both Kansas Cities, we returned to Omaha and the grandparents to rest and regroup. We got Easter dresses and hats when we were in Omaha, or new shoes. Pictures taken when we were away from Omaha show us kids outside in various combinations of diapers, underpants, and baggy sunsuits tied at the shoulders, standing with other suspicious-looking, needful children, squinting or shielding our eyes from the sun, in bare dirt yards. My grandfather took some of these pictures with his big sportswriter's camera, and I can't help wondering what he saw when he looked at us through that lens, waiting for the flashbulb to go off so he could reload the film and fix another bulb. Love, certainly, for he adored us, but he had to be afraid for us, worried at least. Everyone was so young.

My father was an angry, violent man. We moved around so he could finish his education, but his self-image as an urbane academic, a historian, didn't jibe with the reality of the family constellation. We lived on what little money my mother could make as a secretary, and the violence in our ersatz homes was palpable and escalating. Dinners became creamed hamburger on toast with a little violence on the side. Rage simmered with the bullybeef; chili was dished up along with a big scoop of humiliation.

My memories of that long-ago time are blessedly fuzzy, but the feelings, if not the details, come back with great clarity if I concentrate. We're at the dinner table, the baby in a high chair, my sister and I sitting on upended suitcases. Dinner is canned chili, some greasy off-brand, the meat fatty with occasional pieces of gristle or bone. My sister takes a bite and gags. "Chew," my father says, and my sister swallows the bite in one gulp. "Again," says my father, and when she gets another bite in her mouth, "Chew." She gags and swallows, and my father sends her flying off her suitcase with a swift backhand. Maybe it's me who goes flying, a welt rising on my forehead, a goose-egg from his big class ring. Maybe it's my mother this time, and it breaks the chair, and that's why we're sitting on suitcases. Maybe the baby in the high chair is the one who is slapped because she's afraid, and confused about what chew means, or what it means to swallow.

Here is the recipe:

Bullybeef with Rage (Unrestrained)

Brown 1 pound hamburger with one chopped onion. Drain grease and add a large can of tomato sauce. Mix with one package cooked macaroni. Add salt and pepper to taste.

Serves six to six hundred, depending on how much macaroni is used.

I remember spending holidays at my grandparents' house, and they were all centered around the big meal. Ham at Easter, hot dogs and hamburgers during summer holiday picnics, and turkey with all the trimmings at Thanksgiving, trimmings that included canned cranberry sauce and the ubiquitous Jell-O salads: lime Jell-O with marshmallows, black cherry Jell-O with pineapple chunks and grated carrots, orange Jell-O with a dollop of Cool Whip. Mincemeat pie, cake from a boxed mix, perhaps embellished with coconut, or too-green candied citron.

One of Grandma's experimental Jell-O salads became enshrined in family lore when my sister dubbed it "barf salad," rudely, at the Thanksgiving table. Grandma was eventually jollied out of hurt feelings, and we kids insisted it be served at every Thanksgiving thereafter.

While musing about barf salad, I called my mother in Omaha to get the recipe.

"Oh, God," she said. "I don't have that recipe . . . Hold on, wait a minute."

After a while, she got back on the phone. "I've got a cookbook that your grandma made for Christmas gifts one year . . . Okay, here it is," and she read me the recipe. We laughed so hard, we cried.

"Barf" Salad

2 pkg. lemon Jell-O
1 #2 can crushed pineapple
4 oz. can pimiento—seed and cut up
¾ cup nuts
½ lb. American cheese (grated)
1 cup whipping cream (whipped)
2 Tbsp. Mayonnaise

Dissolve Jell-O in 1 cup of water. Add pineapple juice. Set until syrupy. Stir in rest then fold in whipped cream. Serve chilled on a bed of iceberg lettuce.

"Your grandmother typed each one of these recipes over and over on your grandfather's old typewriter," my mom said. "Oh, my, here's a recipe for pork scrapple . . ."

We laughed and gagged over the cookbook for a while, and then she offered to mail it to me.

A few days later, the cookbook arrived. I opened the yellow envelope and the smell of stale cigarette smoke hit me in the face. My mom sent a note, letting me know she'd included a few Post-its for "edification/humor," and that she didn't try to clean the cover, instead deciding to leave the "flavor" on.

I settled in at my desk to study the book. Covered with gaudily flowered contact paper in the harvest gold, avocado, and burnt orange colors popular in 1970s kitchens, the book, a small three-ring binder, was tabbed *Casseroles Etc.*; *Desserts*; *Candy*; and *Salads.* The cover page read *"Merry Christmas 1971: Old and New Family Recipes."* Only two recipes were included in the candy section (*Penuche* and *Peanut Brittle*), and one of the salad recipes was called *Aunt Alice Elliott's Dessert or Salad.*

Some of the pages were stuck together by splatters of Grandma Sib's *Dilly Casserole Bread* ("Gram used to bring this to all the family gatherings," my mom's Post-it read), Grandma Meier's *Southern Pecan Pie*, and Aunt Nome's *Good Dip for Vegetables.* There was another note on the recipe for brownies: "She was the wife of the minister that taught me to drive." Most of the recipes were horrid: the main ingredient for *Simple Chicken Delight* is cream of chicken soup; the first ingredient for *Heavenly Cake* is a seven-ounce jar of marshmallow cream. A Post-it note on a recipe for *Texas Cake* mysteriously read, "This was a very big deal in the 60s."

By this time, I was so amused I had to share some of the recipes with Jeff. He listened as I read recipes and shared stories, wiping tears away as I laughed. Suddenly, I sat up straight.

"Oh, my God," I said. "This is the recipe *that I* use for turkey stuffing!" Although I've modified it, substituting real wild rice for Uncle Ben's and using fresh herbs, sure enough, it was the same recipe I'd been using for years. I didn't remember it as a family recipe, and was stunned and embarrassed to see it in the book.

By the time Jeff and I got together, I was already a pretty good cook. I had cooked my way through my lonely and unhappy first marriage. The cooking, in addition to bringing pure pleasure and sustenance, helped ground me when things got bad. It served me, and us, well when we blended a family of four children who were all wounded by divorce. When bad things happened, I fed them. When our children returned distraught and agitated from visitations, while they acted out or collapsed into exhausted heaps, I fed them. I introduced them to new things and fixed their favorite dishes. Good cooking marked our holidays and our celebrations. I cooked to keep the rhythm of family life beating, and when things were difficult, sometimes I cooked so I could *move*. Cooking brought me out of the paralysis and through the brittleness of pain.

I cooked through first dates, first periods, and occasional misdemeanors. First dates require steaks for the boys, for energy and courage; and salads for the girls, to maintain the figure and prevent gas. Omelets for the periods. Jail food for the little criminals: bean soup, baloney sandwiches and orange drink. Sopa de Lima, Mexican Lime Soup, for Jeff, to settle his stomach and catch his tears when he returned from the airport without his children, even though the dates were agreed to and the tickets purchased. The Blue Plate Special, meatloaf, mashed potatoes and peas, to try to comfort my son when his friend died. No matter the cause or level of the seismic upheaval, we had to stop: dinner was ready, it was time to eat.

I cooked through plenty of hilarity, too. One night, Maggie, by then a teenager, was getting dressed for the prom, and her date came to the door. Jeff and I invited him in, and we sat at the kitchen table waiting for her to emerge. I found the table at an antique store. Some people call it a refectory table, but it's a draw leaf, made of oak, with ends that pull out and up. It is the same kind of table that my grandparents had in their kitchen, where I learned to dunk my toast.

Maggie walked down the hall and entered the kitchen. She was stunning and voluptuous in a coral-colored, satin dress. High heels covered her feet and hid her toes, bloodied from playing lacrosse.

The date's eyes opened wide, and then he nervously looked down at his lap.

The smile on Maggie's face faded, and then her face crumpled. "Aren't you going to say anything?"

The date stuttered and stammered until finally he blurted out, "I like them!"

"You like them?" Maggie said incredulously. "What's that supposed to mean?"

Jeff's eyebrows were working overtime as she spun around and ran back down the hall.

The date started hitting himself in the head with the heels of his hands. "I'm such an idiot!" he said, banging on his forehead. "I always say the wrong thing!"

Gently, Jeff started talking to him. "Next time, just say 'You look nice.' That always works . . . You need to go back and talk to her."

I got up from the table as the date walked down the hall. I gave Jeff an oh-my-God look and started skewering the shrimp that had been marinating in a bowl. I had to stuff a dish towel in my mouth to keep from laughing. After the kids left, Jeff and I howled with laughter as we relived the scene, holding each other up to keep from falling down in laughing puddles. We laughed as we grilled the shrimp, laughed as we ate it, and laughed for a long time after the meal was finished.

"I like them," Jeff would say, and we'd be at it again.

"You look nice," I said as we drifted off to sleep.

∼

Jeff calls our blended family a "blendered" family. Our domestic life was constantly agitated by ridiculous, hurtful, and unanticipated interferences by the children's other parents. We held on tight to keep the lid on.

The details of my own childhood are unimportant. The recalling or telling of it brings me no relief or catharsis. There is nothing instructive in the story. There was really no redemption, and while there have been endings, they haven't been all that happy. My childhood, processed, absorbed, and mostly overcome, provided me no ability to protect my own children from theirs, even though I tried with all my might. I had the insight, but lacked the skills to fix things for them.

Time doesn't really heal wounds, at least not wounds this ancient or this deep. What time does is help you carry the wounds; it helps you learn to wear them. The wounds themselves remain sharp and bloody, even though they're covered and contained like a pearl. A big enough jolt can cause the pearl to crack, unleashing the jagged and bloody pain. The wounds are monsters, savages, bent to destroy self and others. I learned this when my mother was dying and all of us, my brothers and sisters, turned around to see our sad childhoods leering back at us.

Even then, I cooked to maintain some sense of equilibrium.

"We don't usually eat like this," my sick mother said when I was making one of many dinners at her house while I was taking care of her.

I put my forehead against hers, looked into her eyes playfully, and said, "You do your therapy, I'll do mine."

It was instinct, not habit, that pushed me to cook and led me to establish and maintain the family rituals that mostly involved food. I'm irresistibly drawn to the relics, the kitsch, and the feeling of times that have passed. I was able to remember and draw on the good things, and to somehow know that they matter. I nourished my family with good food, and plenty of it. At least I could do that, and it mattered. It's what drew me to Chautauqua Lake. I understand now that I've had to reach through my parents to my grandparents to learn how to live like a human being. I hold on to the rituals, and to my draw leaf table. We moved walls and doors so the table would fit into the kitchen of our new home.

My children are all young adults now, and still want me to cook for them. They call me for recipes and cooking tips. It gives me great pleasure when they request chicken enchiladas with green chili sauce, zucchini pancakes, or sweet corn salsa. They are adventurous and sophisticated eaters.

Just the other day, Maggie, an adult now, called me from a grocery store. I was driving.

"Mom, I'm going to try making steaks with a gorgonzola sauce. Do I get sweet or dry sherry?"

"You can use any kind of wine," I said. Then I rattled off instructions and ingredients: Cook the steaks in a little olive oil and set in a dish to warm. Add a little more oil to the pan and sauté shallots and garlic. Turn the heat up, pour in a little broth and let the sauce reduce . . .

"Mom!" she said. "My recipe says to do exactly the same thing! How did you know?"

"The same way I know that you need ground beef to make hamburgers," I said, reminding her of a grocery store call she'd made to me a few years ago.

The cooking started out as an obligation that I tried to make the best of, and became a comfort to me, and to them. But as I worked my way through the Mexican phase, Italian phase, and Cajun phase, dabbled in Indian, Moroccan and Middle Eastern, and moved into French, it blended together and became art.

The fall after our mother died, I went to see my sisters. They live in Madison, Wisconsin, on Lakes Mendota and Monona. I left the beauty of Chautauqua behind and drove through barren plains, around Gary, Indiana, and industrial Chicago. As I entered Wisconsin, the topography changed as I drove by green fields, rolling hills, and rust-colored marsh plants, into territory that reminded me of my own home with its gentle beauty and watery nature.

My sisters and I grew closer while we negotiated the complicated terrain of caring for our dying mother in a place that was heavy with ancient and unfathomable history, a place that dragged our bodies and spirits down, an oppression that entered our bones. We expended more energy than was healthy worrying about and trying to soothe each other. Sometimes our monsters were unleashed as we lashed out over ancient wounds that were not of our own making, but mostly it was just hard, and we found our ways through. We drank too much but could not quench our thirsts. We were so thirsty.

We still hadn't gone through the pictures and trivial things that we'd saved after our mother died, so we dove in, my sister's dining room serving as a staging area. When we were too exhausted, sad, or confused to look at another picture, we looked at their lakes, or talked about mine. We were baptized by fire, but all of us, in one way or another, have gone to water. We've found a new source in cool water, purification in cold weather. One of my sisters has a table like mine, a draw leaf, just like the old kitchen table of our childhoods.

In addition to the pictures, and the worthless mementos that remained of our grandparents' and mother's lives, there were boxes and boxes of recipes, mostly awful, and they provided much-needed comic relief. Here's one:

Banana Salmon Salad

3 bananas, diced
½ cup canned pineapple, diced (about 2 slices)
1½ cups canned salmon
¼ cup diced celery
½ tsp. salt
1 Tbs. chopped pickle
Mayonnaise to moisten

Mix bananas and pineapple together. Add flaked salmon. Fold in remaining ingredients. Garnish with crisp lettuce and lemon slices. Serves 8.

The holiday meals are at my house now. For Thanksgiving, I make a fresh turkey, never frozen. Dressing with wild rice, fresh herbs, and a little sauerkraut, to keep it moist and add a little zing. It's an old family recipe from that awful cookbook. Creamed spinach, pumpkin rolls, Julia Child's apple clafouti, green beans with sausage and onions, mashed potatoes and gravy, fresh cranberries instead of canned. I serve the food on a maple dining room table that belonged to my father's parents, and extend the seating with my draw leaf table, the kind of table my mother's parents had. During the rest of the year, the draw leaf table is in my kitchen nook where we eat our breakfast. I watch the birds, and dunk my toast in my coffee, even though Jeff thinks it's kind of gross.

Karaoke Night at the Casino

Try a little tenderness.

—Otis Redding, Percy Sledge, Aretha Franklin,
Three Dog Night, and a whole bunch of other people

In the summer and on into the fall, Thursday night is karaoke night at the Village Casino. The Casino isn't a casino at all. It's a restaurant and bar on the spit of land where the ferry runs, connecting Bemus Point and Stow. For centuries, the Seneca, the Iroquois, and other tribes of the Five Nations met on this point, before a Pittsburgh steel magnate purchased it in the early 1900s.

The basic structure of the Village Casino is still the same as when it was built in 1930. A large dock with boat slips faces Stow, and boaters can walk from their boats to the big deck, filled with tables, umbrellas, and colorful planters. Duck nests are buried in the flowers that run along the railings. Inside is a large, terraced room with tables and chairs, a bar, ice cream and take-out counter, bandstand, and pinball arcade. The owners recently remodeled the main level, replacing the old wood flooring and carving out a gift shop. Off the main room, doors open onto a little city park with swings, playground, and basketball court, and upstairs is the dance hall.

Today, they occasionally have dances upstairs, mainly for teens and tweens, but in its heyday, in the 1930s and '40s, the joint was jumpin'. All the big bands played there: Tommy Dorsey, Glenn Miller, Harry James, Count Basie, Benny Goodman. Sammy Davis, Jr. and Cab Calloway played there, too, and Frank Sinatra, when he was doing his Catskills gigs in the early days and meandered west toward Buffalo and Cleveland. Tickets were two or three dollars a couple, and sometimes were marked $1.50 a person, or Men, $1.60, Ladies, $.40. Some newer bands started at the Casino before they hit the big time, too: Rusted Root, and 10,000 Maniacs, whose lead singer, Natalie Merchant, hails from Jamestown.

As a rule, I hate karaoke. Before the Casino, I'd only experienced it reluctantly, when I was dragged into a bar by acquaintances during a business trip in Atlanta. Confronted by techno music and strobe lights, I felt assaulted by the screeching voices of young people who had obviously had too much to drink. I don't understand people who are into karaoke, and am a little suspicious of them, like I'm suspicious of people into line dancing or scrapbooking. In this place, though, even the karaoke is tinged with nostalgia, infused with a bit of tenderness.

We discovered karaoke night accidentally. I had driven to the lake with the girls, and we arranged to meet Jeff at the Casino for a late dinner when he was able to break away from work to make the drive from Delaware to join us. He called me from his cellphone when he was getting close so I could order his food, and arrived just as the waitress was serving our dinners. We'd just begun to catch up when the music started. We were captivated as people, alone or in groups, took the stage and sang. Some people were terrible, most were average, and some were quite good. But it was Henry, an older man who sang Sinatra, who hooked us, and after that we went to karaoke night as often as we could.

Not long ago, Jeff and I arrived at the Casino a little late, and the place was packed. We put our name in with the hostess, but the chances of our getting a table looked hopeless. The menu consists of adequate bar food, including a wide variety of sauces to accompany the Buffalo wings. In 1985, the Casino made the *Guinness Book of World Records* for serving the most wings in a twenty-four hour period. The hostess finally signaled us. Just as we settled into our seats and got ready to order our food, the music started.

A couple of people went on stage, and they were too unremarkable even to laugh at. We sipped our beer and suffered through; after all these years, we knew that Henry was worth the wait.

Finally, the karaoke guy called for Henry, and helped him climb the steps up to the stage. Henry was in his seventies; maybe even eighty. With white hair and glasses, dressed in a polo shirt, khaki slacks, and boat shoes, he looked like a retired middle manager, or teacher. He modestly made his way to center stage, adjusted the mike, and the music started.

As soon as he hit that first note, though, Henry became Frank Sinatra. He snapped his fingers and moved with ease as he came in off the beat, a little early or a little late, and every note, every lyric, was perfect. The phrasing and the tone rang true. He does Perry Como and Tony Bennett perfectly, too, but when it's "The Summer Wind," or "I've Got You Under My Skin," he's simply Frank. He looked at the crowd openly, with no airs, and never glanced at the monitor that flashed the words, follow-the-bouncing-ball-style, to both the singer and the audience. He didn't embellish or change things. Henry was Frank Sinatra. He hit it, nailed it, and was pure understatement, perfection, and grace.

When Henry sings, the summer tourists are recognizable by their raised eyebrows, open mouths, and general looks of astonishment. If they're with someone who knows him, they get an elbow jab, a look, and maybe a whispered I-told-you-so. The rest of us, the regulars, are Henry's fan club. We chitter before he goes onstage, and clap, or stand up and clap an ovation when he's finished. On a typical night, Henry does three or four songs, perfectly, with Frank's inimitable elegance and style.

Years before, when she was still healthy and able to travel, we brought Jeff's mother to karaoke night. The place was packed. Large tables were occupied by families: little kids, teenagers, parents, and grandparents, talking, laughing, eating. Adults drank beer and kids had Cokes, waiting for the music to start. The mood was festive and raucous, and when the music started, people danced. Fathers danced with toddlers, sisters danced with each other, and a shy boy, about fourteen, reluctantly hit the dance floor with his grandma. He learned something that night, about rhythm, grace, and the movement of women's bodies.

"This place reminds me of Montana," Jeff's mom said, a big grin on her face.

I remembered fiddlers' contests in Montana, where generations gathered for the party, to dance and listen to homegrown music. Informal gatherings, where the normal rules of society were relaxed, and everyone acted all right anyway. Jeff's mom tapped her feet and clapped her hands in time with the music, but when Henry launched into "The Lady is a Tramp," her eyes misted over. The Casino itself had thrown her back to Montana, where she'd lived for a time when Jeff was a young adult, but Henry threw her back further, perhaps to when she was a young woman, wearing fancy shoes, dancing, and working in New York City before she married.

My own mother, visiting with one of her girlfriends, reluctantly agreed to a karaoke night, too. Once the music started, they both caught the spirit of the place. When Henry sang, the audience was riveted, and as he concluded his song, my mother let out a loud whoop, barely audible over the wild applause. Afterward, she talked about Henry as if he were her own. She claimed Henry as she claimed Sinatra, an icon of her generation. His voice was in the background during pivotal moments when these women were young. Sinatra played as they learned to drive, learned to dance, and fell in love. Henry's singing brought her back to that place and time.

Mostly, Jeff and I tolerate the other singers while we wait for Henry, but that night, after Henry sang, some old cowboy dressed in a Western shirt and scuffed boots shuffled shyly to the stage. He surprised us with a great Merle Haggard, when we'd never have guessed he was an Okie from Muskogee. A peripheral member of a rough-looking group climbed the stage, dressed in camo and combat boots, with a shaved head and shifty, unfathomable eyes. He looked like a survivalist, an escapee from a mental hospital, or a serial killer, but when the music started, he did a wonderful rendition of "Blue Suede Shoes."

Henry took the stage one more time that evening. He looked at the crowd, his eyes slightly magnified by his glasses, and motioned to the karaoke man that he was ready. Once the music started, he was transformed, and carried us with him as he flew us to the moon. After the song, he gingerly descended the steps to the floor and returned to his life as a retired middle manager, or teacher. On Sunday, Henry will take his place with the rest of the baritones in his church choir. He'll pass the time doing yard work, cleaning the garage, or maybe watching a ball game or two on TV until Thursday rolls around again when, for a few more minutes, he'll be Frank Sinatra.

There is something difficult to convey about karaoke night at the Casino. In the middle of the sunburned girls who scramble off their boat to do a rendition of "It's Raining Men," complete with hand movements, the boys who are hoping to get lucky in their "Love Shack," and the fat bartender in his tight T-shirt, which he pulls up to show his belly as he mugs and struts and does Jagger, a kind of gentle love sometimes comes poking through. Something sweet, a tiny miracle.

Perhaps it's the old-fashioned sensibility at the lake that lets this happen. There is a lack of cynicism here, an underlying warmth that gently radiates like the soft summer light. It's a pull that makes sullen teenagers come awake and stop being snotty when they're fishing off the dock, skiing, or tubing, and later, when they forget themselves and their cellphones, enjoying the fire pit or simply walking the lanes in Maple Springs. It's what makes children, tethered tightly and perhaps overly managed at home, become regular kids again. Here they play pirates and unorganized ball, they shoot hoops, ride bikes, find shells, walk creek beds, explore. They decorate their bikes for the Maple Springs Fourth of July Parade, and climb on the fire trucks after the parade is over. They make brownies for the Labor Day picnic. If they're lucky, they go to karaoke night at the Casino with their parents and grandparents.

People, including me, are a little tenderer here. It's in this place, on this beautiful lake, that Jeff and I are learning to live our lives with more openness, reverence, and grace. Henry represents something of this to me. The spirit of the lake somehow seems to draw us in and wash over us. In this lovely place our veneer is stripped and our varnish softened, just like the old boats.

Falling Down

When you feel like you've hit bottom, you know, you're really on your way up. You just don't realize it yet.

—Scott Kovel, our neighbor in Maple Springs

It is impossible for me to decide which is more difficult: recognizing and preparing for an inevitable and significant loss, experiencing it, or recovering from it. I can track the losses; we have dates on the calendar to prove them. The recovery part is much more blurry. For so long, a little burst of recovery was inextricably entwined with more grief. We were submerged, drowning.

Even after all this time, I have difficulty recalling what came first, what came last, what the middle of it was like. Things were topsy-turvy, out of order, almost as laughably ridiculous as they were excruciating. I want to be able to say that first this happened, and then this, and finally, this, but it wasn't like that. It was unbearable sadness piled on top of jarring pain, mixed with grueling work, marked by confusion and disorientation. We lost our bearings and couldn't find our joy.

My joke is that Jeff's mother moved in with us fifteen minutes after the last kid moved out, but I'm only half kidding. Initially, dementia made it impossible for her to continue to live alone, so we moved her into our home soon after the last child moved away. We made a nice apartment for her in the basement. She had dinner with us, but could get her own breakfast and lunch, and we could leave her occasionally for a lake fix. When a woman has only sons, her care often falls to a daughter-in-law. She and I loved each other and shared a lot of laughs. It helped when things got rough, as they often were. Of course living with her was a strain for all of us. It was sad helping her come to terms with those things she was losing: independence, driving, managing her own money. "Go ahead and cry," I said to her one evening. "You have a lot to cry about." And later, "Let it go. Raise your arms and dance. Jeff will manage your checkbook and pay your bills."

Our privacy was invaded. And although she could usually be teased out of bad moods, she was an early riser and greeted each day with a complaint. It got to us—we're happy people in the mornings. I tried to shake off the depression that closed in around me and accept the ways that my own life shrank as the space she occupied in it grew. Anyone who has lived with an aging parent knows that feeling of constant wariness and worry. It's different from worrying about children who ideally grow into independence. It's backward, watching the decline instead of the blossoming, waiting for yet another shoe to drop, the proverbial first shoe having dropped long ago.

After a fall broke Jeff's mother's pelvis, she moved into an assisted-living facility. I spent countless hours in emergency and hospital rooms with her for falls, pneumonia, nascent strokes, broken bones, and a near exsanguination brought on by blood thinners. The dementia that precipitated our need to care for her continued to worsen. After one of her falls, she cut her leg badly, and then developed a dangerous MRSA infection. The doctors decided to operate. Jeff and I spent all day with her in a quarantined room, fully gowned and gloved. When she seemed settled, we went home. As soon as I crawled in bed after that exhausting day, the hospital called to tell us she was hallucinating, and if someone didn't get back up there quickly, they were moving her to the psych ward. I grabbed my toothbrush and nightie, and spent the rest of the night in her hospital room, trying to calm her and keep her in bed, quarantine procedures forgotten.

That night was Christmas Eve, and right after New Year's, still on tenterhooks about Jeff's mother, I got that dreadful call that my own mother had terminal cancer. It wasn't fair. Busy with Jeff's mother, I assumed I would have more time with my own later, and so did she. We thought we had more time.

My sisters and I began the difficult job of caring for our mother long-distance. We took turns, sharing two- or three-week stints in Omaha, overlapping when we could to orient the sister who was on duty next. Each of us was careful not to burden the sisters who weren't "on deck," even though it was impossible to rest even when we were home. "You have to talk to me," was our code to signal an emergency, a crisis, or some crazy thing that a caregiver couldn't figure out on her own. The code meant, "You have to talk to me."

Our family history meant that each of us had a complicated relationship with our mother, and I suppose everyone does. Maybe it's easier for people who have sweet little old white-haired mothers, but somehow I don't think so. There was nothing easy about the endless doctors appointments, the waiting rooms filled with other people's suffering, or the nausea, the constipation, the dehydration. Nothing easy about the discomfort, or the pain. My mother's bones hurt, even though nothing showed up on the scans. There was nothing easy about the port they inserted for chemotherapy, or the excruciating pain my mother had before they figured out the port was inserted incorrectly. There was nothing easy about the stroke my mother had in her arm, or when her friends came over and they shaved her head, or the wasting weight loss, or the seizures. There was nothing easy about this dying, this death.

"How's your mom?" Jeff's mother would ask when I'd visit her in her room after a stint in Omaha.

"She has cancer," I'd say.

"Oh, I'm sorry," Jeff's mom would say. She didn't remember that I had told her about my mother on numerous occasions. Her dementia made her relive the moment over and over, like it was always fresh. She didn't remember that her brother had died, either, even after she posted yellow sticky-notes all over her room as reminders.

Although he tried to protect me from it because I was drowning in caregiving and grief, Jeff himself was busy trying to save his business. He'd started a retail construction company years before with an initial investment of seven thousand dollars, four of which was borrowed. He quickly moved from loving the building of things to loving the business of things. He built the business up with his own hard work, and had survived big economic swings before. But when the economy soured in 2009, Jeff's work started slowing down. Retail construction slumped, then stalled. Finally, the comfort of his receivables column turned into an unnavigable sea of red ink when one of Jeff's major clients filed for bankruptcy and would not pay for the stores he had built, even though Jeff had paid for the materials and labor.

Early that July, Jeff picked me up from the airport after I returned from a long, sad stretch in Omaha. He looked awful, and I'm sure I did, too. We went into the house and I started rummaging through the kitchen to see if there was something I could cook. I put chicken in the microwave to thaw, pulled out a bag of frozen lima beans, and made a quick dressing of sesame oil and pomegranate vinegar for a salad. Jeff opened a beer and pulled up a stool at the kitchen counter.

"I've decided to close my company," he said. "I'm going to have to shut it down."

I froze, and then turned to face him. He wore an expression of stunned sadness, and a look I'd never seen on him before. I was watching the man I loved come to terms with powerlessness and defeat.

"Oh, Jeff," I said. "Are you sure?"

"Yeah, I'm sure," he said. "I can't figure out how to keep going. We just lost too much money when I didn't get paid for those jobs. And there's nothing coming in the door."

"I'm sorry," I said. "I don't know what else to say." We just looked at each other for what felt like an eternity. His business was not only our livelihood, it was an extension of his very self. For Jeff, his work was not just a means of income; it was a primary vehicle for his self-expression, a place where he could test himself, occasionally flex his muscles. It was his connection with the larger world, a place where he knew the rules and had some sense of control. Despite the economic strides of women, including their own wives, men like Jeff define themselves in relation to commerce. For Jeff, success in commerce was a measure of his masculinity—not how much money he made, but how he conducted himself and how others viewed him. His competency, his fairness, his ability to solve problems—these were the important things, along with being able to provide for his family.

"Are we going to lose the house?" I asked.

"I don't know," he said. "I have to shut it down is all I know. It's the only way I can figure out how to try to avoid bankruptcy. Of the business, and of us. It's bad, and I don't know how bad it's going to get."

When dinner was finished, I went out on the porch to try to collect my thoughts. After a time, I went back in to talk to Jeff. He was sitting in a chair, but I couldn't tell if he was awake or asleep, he was so bent by the weight of his world. It was a posture he'd held for months. When I got in front of him, I could see that his eyes were open.

"I don't want to be poor," I said. "But I know how to be poor. We'll just get through this." It made me feel better to say it—to name it—but I don't think it really helped Jeff. Nothing did.

In a few short weeks, at the end of July, despite the interventions and before they said she would, my mother died. We were scheduled to go home the day after the funeral. Early that morning, when we were just beginning to stir, Jeff's phone rang. It was the assisted-living facility, letting him know that *his* mother had had a stroke, and that the ambulance was on the way. They put her on the phone, and I could hear her babbling gibberish, even though Jeff had the phone pressed to his own ear. After quick goodbyes with brothers, sisters, and children in Omaha, we rushed to the airport. We couldn't get an earlier flight, but we did manage to make an earlier connecting flight. We got to the hospital ahead of schedule, but our bags stayed on their original flight, and we had to retrieve them later. My bag held my mother, or at least some of her remains, in a Tupperware container wrapped with duct tape, along with a letter from the funeral home, required these days because of heightened airport security.

Jeff's mother spent a couple of days in the hospital, and then transferred to a rehabilitation facility. I flew back to Omaha to begin working with my siblings to sort through all the things that remained from my mother's life. When I returned, Jeff's mother was back in assisted living, although she was at the highest care level they could provide. Jeff and I went to see her.

"Beth just got back from Omaha," Jeff said as we were visiting.

"Oh, how's your mom?" Jeff's mom asked.

"She's dead," I said, even though we had told her before.

"Oh, I'm sorry," Jeff's mother said, and she meant it. We sat and visited for a few more minutes. During the conversation, Jeff's mom asked me where I'd been.

"Omaha," I said.

"Oh, how's your mom?" she asked.

"She's dead," I said.

"I'm sorry," Jeff's mother said.

I looked at Jeff. "I have to get out of here." Although I wasn't the one with dementia, each time the conversation turned, I felt fresh grief.

Jeff closed the doors on his business on a Friday in September, but shutting the business down took months. Every day meant that Jeff had to wade through its decimation and destruction as he sifted through the last twenty years of his life, saying goodbyes, making final payments. I was trying to reclaim my own life and taking care of Jeff's mom. After months filled with confusion and despondency, we decided to move to the lake permanently. If we never regained our footing, at least we'd be in a place we loved.

We put our home and the townhouse on the market and hunkered down to wait. Miraculously, we sold our house in a week. Like everyone else, we lost money, but we got out and were grateful. Selling the house so quickly meant that we would move into the townhouse while we searched for a permanent home at Chautauqua and waited for the townhouse to sell. I was relieved. I was so afraid it would go the other way—that we'd sell the townhouse and be stuck in our primary home; that we'd never be able to get back to the lake. We would move into a townhouse that was perfect for weekend getaways, but that would be a tight squeeze for us and our dog, Henry.

A rescue mutt, Henry is a farm dog, a border collie mix, we think. Jeff named the dog after his dad. Henry is active and hairy, and not suited for quasi-apartment living. We'd adopted him a couple of years before, and always brought him with us when we went to the lake. We walked him often when we were in Maple Springs, both by choice and of necessity, and we'd met a lot of new people because of him. Henry does tricks on command, and will quickly run through his whole repertoire if he thinks he'll get a biscuit out of it. Now he makes neighborhood rounds, and knows exactly where the biscuits are.

We had the usual things to take care of that any move entails, from packing to closing accounts, from filling out change-of-address cards to facing the dust bunnies, and we had to find a new house, a long drive away, in another state. We also had Jeff's ailing mother to contend with.

I listlessly packed and sorted at home while Jeff spent long days in an empty building, sifting through the detritus of his business life. When we could, we broke away for the lake, to house-hunt and to try to find a jolt of joy, a moment of serenity. When we were away, we worried about his mother ceaselessly, and more than once had to leave early to attend to her emergencies.

After another stroke and post-hospitalization stint in rehab, the assisted-living facility reluctantly took her back in, but we placed her on waiting lists for nursing-home care. We started visiting nursing homes, and they were mostly awful. Some sat on lovely grounds, but inside, past the orderly configuration of business offices, was a cacophony of sights and sounds and smells—old people, damaged, in wheelchairs, with walkers, with canes, and some not out of bed. The hallways echoed with mutters and moans and the strained gibberish of those who had forgotten how to speak. Clanging food trays and staff banter intruded upon the oppression, but somehow failed to lift it. Serious injuries and old-age debilitation simplify things—until some healing occurs, everything is simply alimentation and elimination, with a little bit of pain management thrown in. Past the business offices, everything was linoleum and tile and plastic—things that could be wiped down, disinfected, and bleached.

"We need to try to get her into a nursing home at the lake," I said to Jeff one day. The idea had hit me suddenly. Although we had our townhouse, Jeff and I didn't yet feel like residents of Maple Springs. Actually living there was in our future, not in our now.

"You're right," he said. "The signs are not pointing to an admission here."

"I can't believe how dumb we are," I said. "Thinking our only option was to place her here, and then have to drive back and forth to visit her after we move."

Our house-hunting trips now included nursing-home tours. Compared to what we'd seen, the nursing homes here were lovely. We made our final selection after seeing a picture of a neighborhood dog, Sequoia, in the main hallway of one of the nursing homes. Sequoia, a pit bull, is a service dog, very sweet, and our dog Henry's friend at the lake, where they play together often. The Terreberrys regularly brought Sequoia to the home to visit the old people. We figured that a place that loved a pit bull like Sequoia would be a place that would love Jeff's mother, too.

Things weren't going so well on the house-hunting front. Many houses in Maple Springs, and elsewhere on the lake, are cottages, not suitable for year-round living. Affordable houses on or near the lake are often in a state of considerable disrepair, and sometimes are simply beyond repair. We wanted to stay in Maple Springs if we could, but it is a tiny community and sometimes there is nothing available. Period.

A house came on the market during late spring. Close to Rose and Paul's bed and breakfast, it had a wide porch facing the lake, and an attached garage, which is a rarity here, and was in our price range. Inside, it was a disappointment. Over the years, the rooms had been mercilessly chopped up by remodeling. The fireplace, if there was one, was hidden behind remodeled walls, and the kitchen was so dysfunctional that the refrigerator wasn't even in it. Narrow stairs led up to bedrooms with cottage-style painted floors. They were cute, until we noticed the floor had been painted around the beds, leaving big spots of the old paint underneath the legs. A dirt basement contained a mammoth-sized gravity heater. Ancient, it could be removed only in pieces. There was a dock, co-owned with another neighbor, but the lot was crazy. The driveway was actually owned by the neighbor to the right, and the front lawn, nice and deep, didn't belong to the house at all—it was owned by the Whiteside Allotment. Ancient, old-fashioned covenants, and boundaries drawn to suit old railroad and trolley companies must be researched and deciphered before a buyer knows what she'll actually get. Even then, many buyers are surprised when they learn they don't own the lakefront at all and can't even put in a dock after the deal is done.

Another one came available shortly thereafter, and it was on the lakefront. It was listed as a six-bedroom seasonal cottage, and we'd seen enough similar houses to know that six bedrooms in a small cottage meant six crazy rooms radiating off the center of an upstairs "hallway" too small to turn around in. Many seasonal cottages are like that: bedrooms aren't rooms at all, just places to stack beds or put mattresses when the house is overflowing with family or friends. Yards can be too small to park a car or place a picnic table.

We spent the next few weeks mostly apart, juggling the packing and caring for Jeff's mom. That brief period is so muddled in my mind, I can't remember the exact order of things. It was a collision of past, present, and what we hoped for the future. It was a time of great uncertainty, and waiting. Sometime in the middle of it all, we found our house. It was in terrible shape, but the bones of it felt right. It wasn't on the lake. Seeing the beauty of the lake through my sliding doors, feeling the wildness and comfort of the lake, hearing the soothing waves lap on shore, listening to the howling wind, watching the sun set, the moon rise, and the sweep of stars over the lake was what had nourished and sustained me for all these years.

As we weighed our options, I had an epiphany. "If the lake was what was important, we'd be looking for houses all over," I said to Jeff. "What's important is Maple Springs. It's our community."

"We can see a sliver of the lake from the porch of that house," Jeff said. "We can go down there whenever we want. And don't forget, when the summer people leave, the whole lake will be ours."

Jeff's mother's health was declining rapidly, and the date for moving out of our old house was looming. We still weren't certain where we'd land, so by necessity we arranged for a moving company at the lake to ship our household things up here and store them.

Jeff left to finish up the final packing in anticipation of the move. I spent the week at the nursing home. By Wednesday, I knew the time had come for Jeff's mother to leave us.

"You have to come home," I said to Jeff over the telephone that day. "I need you here. I think your mother will be dying soon."

"Okay," he said. "I'll come up tonight. But I have to leave again in the morning to be here for the movers. Or they won't move us."

It's a cliché to say that when one chapter closes, another one opens up, but whoever coined that cliché had something figured right. We lost Jeff's mother on moving-out day. Under the circumstances and against their policy, the movers loaded our household goods, memories, and treasures and then took them to storage without our being there to supervise. Later that week, our offer was accepted on the new house.

We took some of Jeff's mother's cremated remains to Long Point, and threw them into the lake over the side of the boat, near where Butch's retirement mementos and ashes from my own mother rested in the silt. They bloomed in the water like cream blooms in a coffee cup before they disappeared from our sight. Our hearts were too heavy to notice, but things were beginning to lift.

Wrens

How come you can hear a chord, and then another chord, and then your heart breaks open?

—Anne Lamott

Outside the kitchen window of the townhouse, I had two bird-houses. Decorative and kitschy, the first was a gift from my mother-in-law. I hung it up under the eave on my back porch, away from the lake. Since it was designed more for gaudy looks than function, I never expected inhabitation, but to my surprise, the next spring brought a pair of chickadees. I watched them come and go, building their soft nest of moss, lining it with feathers, poking their heads into their house beyond my sight.

When the eggs hatched, Jeff and I watched both parents fly to and fro, beaks loaded with bugs, and could hear the hatchlings peep peep with excitement. In a short time, just days, the babies fledged and the nest was empty again. Then the chickadees returned, tidied up, and raised a second brood.

I hung another birdhouse, prettier and more artistic, next to the tacky one a couple of years later. It was made of teak, with a twisted twig at the entry that served as a roost. The chickadees selected the new house that spring, and the other went empty. By the end of the season, the empty birdhouse looked abandoned on the outside as well. Dusty and covered with webs, it reflected the inside vacancy.

When Jeff and I were involved in the transition of moving permanently to the lake, his mother rapidly declining in the nursing home, a pair of wrens set up housekeeping in the teak birdhouse. I watched them clear out the fuzzy remnants from the chickadees to build a wild and twiggy nest of their own design. I watched them from the kitchen window, and after some scolding, they let me watch from a chair on the porch itself. After spending long hours at the nursing home with his mother, I walked the dog and then sat on the porch, passing lonely time in the evening while Jeff was away managing the other parts of our lives. The lakefront was gorgeous, but I craved the solitude of the back porch. I was tired, and still grieving the loss of my own mother.

The wrens soon arrived with beaks filled with bugs, and we could hear the peep peep of the chicks signaling their arrival. "Feed me, feed me," they chirruped at the top of their lungs.

Wrens are tiny things, smaller than chickadees, but their songs are loud and melodic, joyful and lush. We woke to the sounds of the wrens, and marveled at their labors the rest of the day. They sang while they worked, sang while they built their nest, and sang while they fed their babies.

On the Saturday after Jeff's mother's death, I went out onto the porch, past the nest of wrens, and toward my car to run some errands. I glanced down and noticed a baby bird out of the nest on the hard patio, lifeless. It looked prehistoric, like a small gray dinosaur. No feathers covered its wrinkled flesh. Looking back toward the house, I saw another baby on the steps, still wriggling. I dodged the bird and ran into the house to get Jeff.

"I don't know how to put baby birds back in a nest," Jeff said.

"Neither do I," I replied. "But we're doing it. We have to do it."

I grabbed some dishwashing gloves and we went back out. The patio was complete carnage: five baby birds in heaps, some wriggling, others still. I was horrified. Jeff put the gloves on and took the birdhouse down. Setting the birdhouse on its back, he gently poured the babies back into the hole, and placed one in the garbage can.

I watched from the kitchen window to see what would happen next. A bird, larger than the wren, landed on the birdhouse. A finch, panting, its beak open. The finch had tossed those baby wrens out of their nest to build one of its own. I ran outside and shooed it away, furious for its massacre of those helpless babies, its devastation of my wrens.

I waited and hoped, knowing in my heart that nature wins and that our efforts were bound to be futile. But I couldn't bear to lose those baby wrens, not on that day. I'd had enough of death and loss. In part because they were so close together, each loss was a reminder of the other losses. A new loss doesn't soften the old ones, it magnifies them. A heart can hold a lot of grief.

That day, our grief was fresh and raw. The image of those baby birds on the patio was almost more than I could stand. I guarded the nest for a time, and eventually my wren came back. She stuck her head in the nest, counted the remaining babies and began cleaning house. Before she fed those babies, she cleaned, tossing all the finch remnants overboard onto the porch. Not until the house was clean did she start bringing bugs, stopping occasionally to sing her beautiful song.

Watching the wren work to restore order from chaos reminded me of my own need to create some semblance of order when my sisters and I were caring for our dying mother. As soon as my mother got sick, she was very sick, and needed our help. We took turns being in Omaha, creating complicated calendars and spending weeks away from our own homes to stay with Mom. Between driving her to and from treatments and appointments, fixing meals, and managing medications, we worked to organize our mother's house. At first, we arranged things so we had a comfortable bedroom and a place to retreat when we were there. Then we cleaned closets, scrubbed floors, swept decks, hung birdfeeders, tossed things. We organized the kitchen, cleaned the stove and refrigerator, arranged and rearranged the dishes, wiped down cabinets. We corralled the Tupperware, an ungodly amount of it, scattered everywhere, and put it in its own drawer. We cleaned underneath the sink. We developed systems for paying bills, tracking symptoms, logging the good days and the mostly bad ones. Throughout it all, we struggled to confront the failures, hurts, and extraordinary pain of our childhoods, suddenly looming large, out of mothballs.

I returned home to a clean house after my first two-week stint in Omaha. Jeff had hired a housekeeper to tidy things up. It was a sweet gesture, but I was more comfortable later on, coming home to a house that needed straightening. Doing laundry, cleaning toilets, and mopping floors helped me free my body, stiff and clumsy with grief. I imagined myself one of those syphilitics with *locomotor ataxia*. Carrying grief, my face didn't seem to move right, and there was a tightness, a heaviness, in limbs, back, shoulders, and solar plexus that I couldn't shake. I would pick something up, carry it around, and set it down again, forgetting why I had it in the first place. I wandered aimlessly in circles and could not work my way around my own kitchen. My sisters had the same experience: we called it "doing laps." A tidy closet, a mop bucket, or my hand on the iron, moving it back and forth, smelling the quick steam, gave me at least a momentary feeling that all was right with the world.

Although the wren came back and put things in order, by the next morning the nest was empty. Dead baby birds littered the patio. I took that birdhouse down and was miserable all day.

At dinnertime, I went to the patio to light the grill, and was surprised by the sound of my wren singing. Not a dirge, but her own joyful song. She spent the evening flitting from my neighbor's tree to the remaining birdhouse, the dusty, unused one, and by morning had it swept of its webs. The old chickadee moss was on the porch. Jeff hung the teak birdhouse back up, and she cleaned it as well. Two houses now, ready for occupancy.

Day after day, she sang brightly, calling for her mate, letting him know she was ready. Her voice carried no hint of her loss. She waited, and she sang.

I was waiting, too. We had made the deal on our new house, but would not take occupancy until the end of the summer. Even then, it would take months before we could actually move in. The house fix was beyond cosmetics; it needed an overhaul before it could be lived in. Jeff grew impatient with my anxiety over being unsettled. Things were turning out better than we'd hoped for, and we were certainly comfortable in the townhouse, if a bit squeezed. But it was for sale, too, no longer really ours. What I couldn't express, what he couldn't understand, and perhaps what I didn't understand, is that during the time of our greatest loss, my house came apart, too. It was tossed and scattered, taken away by strangers to be put in storage. The idea of home was only imagined, as hard for me to grasp as a cloud. I tried with all my might to soldier on, but I just couldn't get out from under the grief that had settled on me like a shroud.

I was surprised when one day later that summer, I saw the wren through the kitchen window of the townhouse. She was sitting on the kitschy birdhouse, her feet gripping the outside ledge, her tail inside. Her head was bent as if in prayer, and she was very quiet, very still. I watched her for a while, wondering if she was sick or injured. Then I understood: she might have been praying, but she was in labor, too. I had missed the nesting entirely, but there she was, laying eggs.

Slowly I remembered that it was the one-year anniversary of my mother's death. As my mind swirled, I was riveted by the wren. Watching her, some part of me was aware that I was witnessing something primal and essential on this significant day, although I'm still sorting it out.

A year is what we're given to grieve the loss of someone important, and now I understand some of what creates this seemingly universal cultural norm. It takes a year to get through the major milestones on our calendars—holidays, like Christmas, Thanksgiving, and birthdays—without the loved one. But I needed a year to relive the previous year; each day lived in strange tandem, inextricably tied to the same day the year before. The new days carried the shadow of the old days, together forming some weird barometer of my emotional state. I needed to sort through the order of things, to remember how good I felt before my mother got sick and how badly I felt during, and after. My mind needed to relive the doctor's visit where we saw my mother's body lit up by cancer on a screen, needed to recall my brothers' and sisters' beautiful faces filled with pain, needed to remember the funny things that happened in the middle of it all. It takes a year to begin to emerge from that awful place where unwelcome thoughts, memories, and images appear, swirling around with self-recrimination and, often, self-loathing. Not quite the intrusive thoughts of the truly insane, but perhaps as potent: the unbidden, unavoidable thoughts that come to those of us crazed with grief. It took a year before my hand stopped reaching automatically for my telephone to call my mother, to share something funny or sad. It took a year for my dreams to do the weird and necessary things that dreams do. It took a year for me to muck through my mother's life, and my own childhood, to try to make some sense of it all.

Our parents love us perfectly, but it is imperfectly expressed. Their love has to make its way through their own needs and desires, their circumstances, and perhaps their demons; it has to make its way through their humanity. Her humanity was the reason my mother couldn't protect me from my childhood, and my humanity is the reason I couldn't protect my own children from theirs. As for the wren, nature got in the way in the form of a finch. She couldn't protect her babies either. After all, she was only a bird.

Being so close to so much death in such a short time was difficult, but it was a time filled with mystery, joy, poignancy, and grace. I was struck by the similarities between labor and birth, dying and death, and that was a comfort to me. The dying can be a bitch, but I don't think that death is so bad. The wrens knew something of it, and now, so do I. Our job is simply to keep on living until we can't. All the better if we can sing a little bit in the process.

Watching the wren lay her eggs on that important day helped me understand that the process of nature is our process, too. That little bird was carrying on, doing what birds are supposed to do, despite losing all those babies. And she was singing. As I watched, I realized that it was time for me to carry on, too, and I could feel my grief begin to dissipate. I didn't say goodbye to my mother on that day, but I began to say goodbye to grieving over her loss.

It wasn't long until the wren started feeding her new babies. Their little peep peeps, barely audible at first, grew louder as each day passed. Despite their beauty, or the intensity of the moment, I know that sometimes a bird is just a bird. But those wrens taught me something about grief, and about living. A year after my mother's death and just weeks after Jeff's mother died, they sang to me of their fierce hold on life in spite of the losses. It sounded like bells and flutes and pennywhistles; it sounded like a halleluiah.

Spring

Have a little faith in me.

—John Hiatt

We knew spring was coming because the bitter snow eventually turned to bitter snow mixed with bitter rain. Hyacinths and crocuses, buried under snow, were hidden from our view. When the sun broke through, it was thin and watery, dreary.

In early April spring finally arrived, heralded by the lake thawing just days after I took a picture of Jesse and Jevin Kelderhouse ice fishing together in front of the townhouse. Jesse and I had joked that he would pose in a lawn chair for pictures on the ice, wearing a Speedo, but we never did it. It was gory enough seeing Jesse in a wetsuit, so we figured we could make our fortune selling Maple Springs calendars with Jesse in a Speedo as the centerfold.

The spring was noisy. Before it lay gently with a hint of warmth in the breeze and the soft opening of daffodils, before it pressed heavy with the hot scent of lilacs, the water broke with great cracking contractions. The wind hurled chunks of ice shoreward, and they piled up like misshapen igloos. The sun through the ice walls made a kaleidoscope of colors, captured rainbows in ice.

Although it was beautiful, spring was only percussion. The music of prior springs was missing. One spring we witnessed the thaw, watching ice break up and move with the clouds and the wind. The ice crushed in floes against the beach with breathy heaves, and we could hear it smashing and reverberating as it slammed against Long Point, Bemus Point, and Prendergast, across the lake. That spring, the ice piled up in shattered heaps on the shoreline. From a distance it looked like snow, but closer inspection revealed crystals of ice. The crystals looked as if they'd fallen from chandeliers, broken windows of nouveau and deco glass, symmetrical and sharp. The air was filled with the sound of chimes, tinkling noises composed by ice and wind. When I shoved my hand into an ice heap, it sounded like music, and the crystals fell from my fingers like cold stars.

Jeff said the broken ice reminded him of that scene in the *Superman* movie where the history of Planet Krypton is revealed to the young Christopher Reeve by Marlon Brando. Like Planet Krypton, the history of Chautauqua is embedded in its ice crystals, too. The ice is full of fish and butterflies, birds and trees, Indians, mastodons, stardust, and bats.

Although the music of prior springs was missing, it was as if the lake sent us a clear drumbeat: marching orders to quit sniveling, get moving. It was as if the rhythm of the lake beat fiercely so we wouldn't lose our way. Compared to the delicate crystals of years past, the rough blocks of ice seemed primitive. But they held our mothers, and my grandfather, as he gently washed from the blooms of my irises. They were filled with Butch's mementos,

Spike's youth and old age. They contained our accumulating memories, and when they melted, they released a tiny bit of Jeff and a tiny bit of me.

Spring brought an offer on the townhouse, and then a looming deadline. Ready or not, we would have to be in the new house by the middle of May. Construction progress was slow. It seemed to me that all fall, and all winter, despite improvements to the electrical and plumbing systems, the house kept getting uglier. Everything Jeff touched needed to be completely demolished before it could be fixed, and Jeff touched everything. When we accepted the offer on the townhouse, the kitchen in the new house was down to studs, with the awful, crumbling cabinets crammed onto the front porch that I'd painted long ago. With Jesse Kelderhouse's help, Jeff had opened up the kitchen. Tearing out walls, floor, and ceiling, he began to shape a breakfast nook out of what was originally a porch and pantry, before it was an ugly bathroom and laundry. He took the floor in that area down to dirt, only to discover that part of the foundation had collapsed. Rafters were broken, and floor joists over the kitchen were cracked, some charred by the old knob-and-tube electrical wiring.

The kitchen was awful, but the living room—filled with saw-horses, tools, buckets, and materials—was worse. The filthy carpeting remained. The warped ceiling was still covered by narrow wooden slats that had held up a stained acoustic ceiling. I spent the better part of a week pulling staples and nails out of the ceiling boards. Between that, pulling carpet tacks and nails out of floors, and painting, I'd developed a painful tennis elbow. Jeff hurt his back.

Some days when Jeff went to work on the house, I stayed in the townhouse to pack. Occasionally, I fought to hold back tears.

At times, our forward progress felt like just more loss to me. I stared at the lakefront, burning the view into my mind, determined to take my memories with me when we turned the corner to the new house. I listened to the song of the lake as I watched the stones from the fire pit slowly emerge from the snow, like a backbone out of the earth. The fire pit that would no longer be mine, even though Jeff had touched every stone while he and some of the other townhouse men built it.

On a Saturday in late April, Jeff's phone rang. He was resting on the couch after lunch, before he trudged back to work on the house. I listened as he took the call. I saw the look of concern on his face, and when he mouthed "Jesse," my heart dropped into my stomach.

"Is he okay?" I whispered, interrupting.

Jeff shook his head. He quickly hung up the phone and said, "They just found Jesse. He's dead. He was staying at a friend's house, and they couldn't wake him up."

We went to the visitation at the funeral home. All of the Kelderhouses were there, including Jerry, the missing eldest of Spike's sons, who hadn't been home for sixteen years. Burly and solid like the rest of the Kelderhouse guys, he looked like he'd lived a harder life, so far away from the lake for so long. A television screen flickered in the background, showing slides of Jesse, as the remaining Kelderhouses visited with neighbors and old friends, telling stories and fighting back tears. Many of the summer people turned out for the event, driving from Cleveland, Pittsburgh, Rochester, and Buffalo. The summer community that we now called home is a real community, too, and Jesse held a prominent place in it.

There were pictures of Jesse with fish, Jesse with all of his brothers and sisters, school pictures, photos of Jesse with friends,

Jesse in boats, in water, on ice. There were pictures of Jesse dressed as the Easter Bunny at the annual Easter egg hunt in Bemus Point. I didn't know that Jesse was the Easter Bunny until the obituary came out, but unlike most of the neighbors, I did know he was the chaplain at the V.F.W.

I remembered one late summer morning a few years before when Jeff and I had gone out to the porch to have our coffee. The lake seemed normal, but in the background, underneath the regular sounds of birds chirping, water lapping, and boat motors coughing, we heard a low-frequency hum, insistent, energetic, and relentless. A lake hatch, and we could see fish rise to greet it—midges this time. Lake hatches begin as a miracle. The noise sounds like the Martians have arrived. The insects form columns in the trees, and look like fairies flying in shafts of light that break through the clouds; they look like angels. It isn't until later that they become a plague. Their soft bodies squeeze through screens, land on food, and suffocate those of us who wander into a swarm. Then, as suddenly as they arrive, they're gone. The ground, our porches, and even our living rooms are covered with their carcasses, which quickly turn to dust.

We heard voices, and walked over to join our neighbor Peter Jacoby, who was standing by the road talking with Art Webster. Just then, we saw Jesse Kelderhouse coming toward us from the promenade. He was on an old mountain bike that he peddled around the neighborhood with a plastic grocery bag tied over the seat to keep the stuffing in. He'd tried a new seat, but the old one was more comfortable.

"Hey, guys," Jesse said. He shook hands all around and joined in the conversation.

About that time, Art mentioned to Jeff that he was still a part-time pastor in Westfield, over the hill on Lake Erie.

"I'm the chaplain up to the V.F.W.," Jesse said. We all looked at him incredulously.

"How did you get the chaplain job?" I asked.

"I got elected!" Jesse said with a big grin.

"Do you have to say prayers and stuff?" I asked.

"Yeah," he said. "Oh, but they've got them all printed out."

"That's lucky," I said.

Art chimed in. "So you don't have to go wandering off into some spiritual realm or anything on your own."

While we were all laughing, Art started trying to teach Jesse how to do the blessing, demonstrating the finger positioning and the hand movements.

"This is how you do it," Art said. "In the name of the Father, the Son . . ."

No matter how hard he tried, Jesse couldn't quite do the Benedictine sign. His hands were stiff and inflexible from hard work and injuries. Some of his fingers wouldn't bend the way they were supposed to bend, and others wouldn't straighten out. His pinky stuck out in a permanently awkward position. The harder he tried and the more he clowned, the funnier it got. We all stood there and laughed and laughed, Jesse laughing hardest of all, until Art inhaled one of those darn midges and couldn't quit coughing, even after Pete gave him a pretty good slap on the back.

Art officiated at Jesse's memorial service at the fire hall, our old teacher's desk serving as a makeshift pulpit. Art told the group that he would rather spend time with Jesse than with a lot of the so-called religious people he knew. Jesse's brother Jed reminded us that Jesse was the only person he knew who would eat all your food, drink all your beer, and then pick a fight with you.

Our hearts a little heavier, Jeff and I went back to work on the house, and on the packing. Life went on, although every time I went outside, I thought of Jesse. So did Jeff. Like his dad, Jesse represented something bigger than himself. He was a constant presence on the lake, whether he was mowing, putting in docks and lifts, or just walking on the shore, making sure the lake was okay. He was part of the Kelderhouse legacy, a keeper of the flame. We still seem to catch sight of him out of the corners of our eyes, and anticipate seeing him nod or wave, stop to tell a story, or to share some news.

～

Still missing Jesse, we went into high gear on the house, knowing that we could not get it finished before our deadline. Even when he was in his comfortable world of construction, I could sense a shift in Jeff's bearing. He was wounded. Like Ahab, Jeff had done battle with his Moby-Dick, and he had been hurt. Of course his scars were on the inside, but it seemed if I listened carefully, I could almost hear the clip-clop of that ivory leg. I didn't know if Jeff—used to being the captain of his own ship—would best that whale or be devoured by it. I didn't know if he would find his passion again, his drive. And I couldn't make it better.

We focused on getting bathrooms and kitchen into serviceable order, and making bedrooms habitable. Jeff did the work with the help of a couple of hired men. They hung cabinets, tiled walls, laid countertop, installed lights, built soffits, sanded floors. I followed behind with my paintbrush and cans of Mountain Road, Pussywillow, Baguette, Spiced Apple, and Copper Penny paint.

The day the kitchen stove was installed was a big day. I'd found the stove not long after we found the house, and while it sat, untested, in the Whiting's garage, Jeff had designed the kitchen around it. It's an old Tappan Deluxe, forty inches wide, from the fifties. A large area of porcelain separates the burners, providing additional space for mixing, chopping, or setting hot pans. Two doors flank the large oven door; one holds controls and a space for drying towels, the other a warming rack and space for storing cookie sheets. The high backsplash contains a clock, light, electrical outlets, and a funny old cooking guide, encased inside stylized and chunky chrome. The effect of the chrome makes the stove feel both old-fashioned and sexy, like a vintage Pontiac with a hood ornament.

Thankfully, after a couple of visits from the appliance repairman, it worked. Stoves don't come in that size anymore. Standard stoves are thirty inches wide; commercial models, much more expensive, are available in thirty-six-inch widths. Installing a new stove would have left us with gaps on either side.

I spent the better part of one afternoon cleaning it. I soaked the oven grates in Coca-Cola, and scrubbed them with steel wool. I took steel wool to the drip pans underneath the burners, and to the cast-iron burners themselves. Then I took a clean rag and began rubbing down all the white porcelain with a paste of baking soda. As I slowly rubbed the flat surfaces and curves of that old stove, I was suddenly overcome with memories of my grandmother's stove. I hadn't thought of her stove in forty years, but images of it swam in front of me, through unexpected tears. She'd had a Westinghouse, I remembered, but the style was the same. I remembered my grandmother in her kitchen, pulling a roast out of the oven—beef roast, she called it—lifting the lid off an aluminum pot, steam rising as she checked the potatoes. Beads of sweat formed along her hairline and on her upper lip as she thickened the gravy with flour, grabbing bowls and serving spoons. I remembered the smell of carrots intruding on the meatier smells. Apple pie sat on the countertop as we carried things to the dining room, the last of us moving from the draw leaf table in the kitchen to take our seats for the big meal. Come Lord Jesus, be our guest. My grandfather running his old finger around his plate and sticking it in the baby's mouth, giving my infant son his first taste of solid food, even though the books and doctors said to try cereal first.

I packed and cleaned at the townhouse, too. During breaks, I sat on the lakeside porch, watching spring come to life. As soon as we bought, I had transplanted my grandfather's irises to a bed in the back yard of the new house, replacing one large clump with a rose bush, another with a hydrangea, in the small townhouse garden. As I knelt down to place the bulbs in their new home, I thought about Butch's hands on them, and my grandfather's hands before that, as I covered them gently with soil. I watched the plants I left for the new owners begin to sprout tiny green shoots, a sure sign of life, and hoped my irises would do the same.

We moved ourselves and some of our townhouse furnishings into the house in the middle of May, even though the porch was filled with lumber, doors, and other materials, and in spite of the condition of the living room, which still served as the workshop. I had to leave the birdhouses with the new owners because they were already occupied. The wrens had returned, along with another family of chickadees. Despite the fact that our household furnishings were still in storage, we had everything we needed, and we were grateful. We couldn't move the furniture in until the house was done, so there was still pressure and another round or two of intense work ahead of us, but something else wasn't quite right. It was in the air, but I couldn't grasp it.

One evening, Jeff suggested we try a new wings place on the other side of the lake. The same people who had the Village Casino owned it, and were trying to make a go of it. Jeff had been testy all day, but I was feeling cooped up, so I agreed. We needed a change of scene.

The restaurant was unremarkable. We ordered our wings and the waitress brought us a beer. She was so nice, I started warming up to the place.

"I just love it here," I said to Jeff after she left.

"You don't have to keep saying that," Jeff said. For some reason, my comment had irritated him. Almost everything I said irritated him then. Any attempt I made to make him feel better, or any suggestion I made about our future, caused him to snarl.

"What's the matter with you?" I asked. "You bite my head off over almost everything I say. There's nothing wrong with my loving this place, or expressing it." I fumed for a minute, fighting tears, and then continued. "What I was going to say, Jeff, is that this is the first time in a long time—really, ever in our marriage—that I've had such a sense of community. Of belonging to a community, fitting in."

"Sometimes when you tell me how much you like this place, it feels like you're just putting more pressure on me to get things finished," Jeff said. "Or talking yourself into it liking it, since everything fell apart and we're stuck here."

"I am still anxious and unsettled," I agreed. "Because we are still unsettled. But I'm not trying to pressure you. I like hamlet life, I really do. And you're going to figure out what you want to do."

Jeff sighed. "It just seems like things have been up in the air for so long."

The waitress brought our food. The celery was limp, and the dips were in prepackaged containers.

"We've both been hurt," I said. "But we're making it. You're getting your mojo back, I can feel it. I just want you to be happy, find something that you love doing. I think that's when we'll really turn a corner and start to feel more settled." I took a bite of a greasy chicken wing. "And I'm not sorry that we're here. I'm sorry that things fell apart, but I'm glad we've landed here. Jeff, I'm grateful to be in a place where no matter how tough things get, I feel like looking up. Every day, there's a reason for me to look up. The economy failed. You didn't."

We ate our lousy dinners for a few minutes in silence.

Jeff leaned forward. "You know," he said, "I think it was important for me to spend so much time in our ugly new house. For me to get my hands in it, dig in the ugly, wallow in it. I think it was important for me to take something ugly and make it beautiful."

"You needed the stinky bat nests," I laughed. "Really, though, I think I understand what you mean. We needed to roll around in the muck for a while, really feel and take stock of what we lost. We needed to literally claw our way out."

"With a hammer," Jeff laughed.

"We're not out of the woods yet, Jeff," I said. "But we're not broken. Whether we knew it or not, we've been rebuilding our lives while we rebuilt the house. Now we just need to let each other back in. All the way in. If we do that, the next steps will come, too."

The waitress came back and we paid our bill. The night was cool; nights aren't reliably warm here until July. Jeff took my hand as we crossed the parking lot to the car.

"Let's go paint something," he said.

"Or pound something," I said.

Epilogue

When you come to my house, you'll walk up the stairs onto an open porch. It's still not finished, but the old windows have been removed and are now the windows in the garage we are building. You'll go through a door to enter the enclosed porch. The door used to be Mary and Joe Ferris' door, and before that, it belonged to the Bues, who used to own the same house. The door has been in Maple Springs for a long time. You'll see that the porch is worn, but clean and white, with comfortable old furniture. We can wave to the Whitbecks when they drive by, or to dear Emil Arvidson when he makes his daily trip to the post office. We'll wave to him hard, now that Betty is gone. You'll see the lake from the porch, and will have a better view when the leaves fall off the trees. If you come in summer, a vase filled with gladiolas or sunflowers will be on the table for you. Dried flowers from my hydrangea tree will be in the vase if you come in winter, and in the late summer and fall, the living blooms will press against the window glass.

When you walk through the door into my living room, you'll notice that the paint on the walls, Bakelite Gold, brings out the colors in the wooden trim that surrounds the windows, and offsets the high baseboards. I might tell you that this was the first paint color I chose, and that after we removed two layers of paneling and three layers of wallpaper, we found the same color on the original walls. I might show you a small piece of plaster that I saved so you can see the color, along with the horsehair that held the old walls together.

Your eyes might be drawn to the floor, which is maple, and you'll wonder about the oak insets in the middle of the room. I'll tell you that there were French doors there once that separated the living room from the dining area, and will show you the scar on the floor that looks like an ancient eye, the astragal that held the fixed door in place while the other one was free to swing.

You'll see my old dining room table, a tablecloth covering its worn top, with a window seat behind it. I might tell you it was my grandparents' dining room set, where we once gathered as children to welcome my cousin home from Vietnam, and where those of us who are left gather now that Thanksgivings are at my house. You'll notice the fireplace at the other end of the room, and I will take you to it, to show you the maple leaves that are delicately pressed into the concrete hearth.

You'll notice my furniture, and think it's shabby, or think it's antique, or think it's mismatched, or find it beautiful. I may tell you I've been hauling a three-piece set of mission oak furniture—a settee and two heavy chairs—around for almost thirty years, just waiting for this house, where they belong. If we stay in the living room, you'll sit down and notice a cobweb, or a sprinkling of dust on the mantel, or a puff of dog hair in the corner, or newspapers and magazines spread out on the coffee table. Then you'll slip your shoes off and curl your feet up underneath you, even though you didn't ask, but I won't mind because that's what I want you to do.

Off the living room, through French doors that have stayed with the house, the glass wavy and bubbled with age, you'll see a den. The walls are a deep sage green, and the old trim has been painted white. You'll notice the floors, which are fir, but won't see the holes in them because they're covered by furniture. I may tell you about them; they're holes from sinks where a former owner washed hair in this room, when it was a beauty parlor. I might tell you that the door to a small bathroom used to be the outside entrance to the beauty parlor, and that when we bought the place the door was covered with insulation and opened to nothing. I'll show you the bathroom, but you won't be able to imagine what it looked like before, even if I show you pictures, and you won't be able to smell the bats' nests and hornets' nests that were in the ceiling before we tore it down.

If you come to my house in winter, it might be freezing outside, but you'll be warm. You'll feel the heat come up through old grates in the floor, and you'll stand over them for a minute and remember the feeling of standing over grates like these before, perhaps when you were a child. We'll have a fire. If you come in summer, we'll open the windows, and if we're still too hot, we'll sit in the yard, under the shade of a weeping willow, a pin oak, a variegated birch, or an ancient hemlock tree. We'll have some tea, or maybe some wine, and if you knock your wine glass over and break it, we'll laugh.

When you come to my house, I'll cook something for you on my old stove. You'll smell cinnamon, or rosemary, or cumin, or fresh basil. You'll smell apples, or roasting chicken, or grilled corn.

I'll tell you that the kitchen countertops are made from old bowling alley lanes that we salvaged. If you're interested, I'll tell you it took three men to move them from the trailer to the ground, and then those men cut them to fit in the yard, dragged the heavy pieces into the living room, stripped and sanded them, set them on the cabinets, and finished them in place. I'll tell you that Jeff trimmed the edges with maple because it's hard and resists wear, and because it matches the old maple flooring, full of nail holes from the layers of linoleum, vinyl, and asbestos tiles that used to cover it up.

When you come to my house, you'll see the back yard through the glass doors of the breakfast nook, where my draw leaf table holds our coffee cups, just like the table from my childhood. If you come in May, the yard will be a riot of rhododendrons; in June, you'll smell the lilacs and see my grandfather's irises in bloom, rising tall and purple over the moonbeam coreopsis that's just beginning to bud, a faint hint of yellow. The tree that Mary Ferris gave us when Jeff's mother died might be in bloom, too, a fitting flowering crabapple. If you come in winter, we'll see snow, and lots of it. The bare trees will be beautiful, though, and the hemlock will still be green, and full of birds. We'll see juncos and cardinals, and if we're lucky, we'll see the eagles, or the trumpeter swans in flight.

When you come to my house, I'll take you upstairs and show you to your room. You'll be comfortable there, because you're in a cottage. I'll take you into the bathroom, point out the light sconces that flank the old mirror, and I'll tell you they are from the Whiteside Hotel, the hotel that sat on the lakefront until they tore it down and built the townhouses. I'll tell you that Jeff's brother found them at an auction outside Philadelphia and sent them to us for Christmas, and that Jeff, Jevin, and Jesse Kelderhouse all vouched for their authenticity. Then they talked for a long time about the hotel, and their mom, and their dad.

At some point, you may grow tired of the prattle. When I point out the trim, and how hard Jeff worked on it, and tell you that's why the house feels restored; or when Jeff tells you that all the color and finish choices were mine; or when I tell you that Jeff rebuilt the whole house without a map, without a plan, you might think we're showing off. But when you see Jeff and me exchange a glance, or a gentle touch, it's not about pride of accomplishment, although we have that. It's because even if you saw the house before we started, or in progress, only Jeff and I know what we went through to get here. Only we know the depths of our darkness, and our fear. We alone know how lost we were, how damaged, and that we put our home and our hearts back together with our backs, our arms, and our strong hands.

If you come to my house in summer, we'll walk the lanes of Maple Springs. We'll go fishing, or tour the lake in our old boat. Perhaps we'll have lunch at the Village Casino, or listen to Henry sing. We'll hear the Chautauqua Belle on the lake, and if we see it, we'll wave like idiots. We'll wave at Mat Stage, Rose and Paul's son, who is now the Belle's captain. Maybe we'll walk to the bed and breakfast and have a chat with Rose herself.

If you come in summer, we'll take our towels and books down to the Kelderhouse dock, right where the road bends around the lake. We keep our boat there now. I'll point out the new roof on the shuffleboard, and tell you that the Kelderhouse brothers put it on during the hottest week on record in Maple Springs, after Jesse died. We'll sit around the fire pit in front of the townhouses, or if we feel like it, we'll have a fire in our own back yard.

We'll walk the lanes if you come in winter, too. We'll brave the weather. We'll see the ice fishermen on the frozen lake. Perhaps one of them will be Jevin Kelderhouse, fishing alone. We'll go to

Guppy's on Wednesday for burger night. We'll ski, or read by the fire, or chat, or play a game.

After your visit, Jeff and I will stay, because this is where we live. It's our home. We'll look forward to your return, but we'll be glad to have the place back to ourselves. We'll keep working on this old house, but you'll know that we're okay now. You'll know that our lives are filled more with birdsong than with eulogies, and that our hearts beat in time with the rhythm of the earth here on the lake, under the Chautauqua sky.